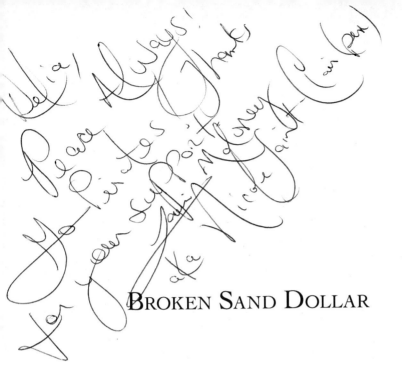

Broken Sand Dollar

Broken Sand Dollar

Finding the Missing *Peace*

Nicole Saint-Clair

iUniverse®

BROKEN SAND DOLLAR
Finding the Missing Peace

iUniverse books may be ordered through booksellers or by contacting:

iUniverse
1663 Liberty Drive
Bloomington, IN 47403
www.iuniverse.com
1-800-Authors (1-800-288-4677)

ISBN: 978-1-4917-8233-0 (sc)
ISBN: 978-1-4917-8234-7 (e)

Library of Congress Control Number: 2016909567

Print information available on the last page.

iUniverse rev. date: 03/08/2017

To families from all walks of life and to caring friendships in all walks of life. Our genuine compassion for one another is the only *thing* we'll ever take with us—when God lovingly, peacefully, and finally calls us home.

Contents

Preface

This book is a suspenseful and harrowing personal journey. Sexual assault and hypnosis are two complicated and controversial subjects within the human condition. This story not only deals with both in an understandable way, but both are interwoven into a personal account that spans three decades.

This writing didn't begin with any religious aspect. In fact, the writing of *Broken Sand Dollar* began solely as therapy. I was trying to make sense of a traumatic ordeal from the past. But as the writing continued, God's presence became inevitable. In looking back, it is now quite clear that He was always there. He sometimes made His presence known in what seemed to be supernatural ways, at the most unexpected times. He is always there for all of us, even in our darkest moments.

I would be remiss if I didn't mention the overwhelming significance of the number three throughout this unusual journey. This number seems to develop its own character with a personality that changes and grows throughout three decades. In the end, the Holy Trinity finally shines through like a glowing light—the Holy Father, the Son, and the Holy Spirit.

This story is based on true events. All personal identities, and some of the places, have been changed for protection. Miracles happen every day. I hope this riveting story will intrigue you, inspire you, and help you understand that God is here for you always.

Most of all, remember that God loves you.

Acknowledgments

Special thanks to my loving husband for your genuine compassion and understanding through this process. This was a long, heartfelt, and oftentimes difficult journey. I am forever grateful for your unconditional love.

Special thanks to my longtime friend who now lives in California. You always listened emphatically, even when you were dealing with your own personal challenges. You were there in the beginning. You are still here in the end.

Special thanks to friends and family members who listened without judging me. This is the most incredible gift that any human being can ever give to another.

Special thanks to God, and to friends and family who have joined Him in heaven since this story began. Thank you for keeping your presence known. Thank you for your eternal love, which gives us all eternal hope.

Introduction

A cool breeze wisped softly around the three of them. The vast sky was a brilliant shade of blue and served as a backdrop to fluffy clouds that scattered into eternity. The three beings floated happily amid the scenery, existing in spiritual form only. In their dimension, no one had an earthly name or an earthly body, yet these three distinct individuals sensed the beauty of nature surrounding them.

The first being, known only as the Almighty One, was ranked higher than the lower two spiritual beings, who were each equal and side by side. The Almighty One was located physically higher as well, soaring across clouds, occupying much more space with its overall presence. They were having a discussion, yet no words were ever spoken. They had no mouths to speak, yet their communication was clear.

"It's time to go now. You've waited far too long," the Almighty One said to the first spiritual being. There was no impatience in its tone, but the message was strong and powerful.

The spiritual being replied, "With all due respect, I'm not ready for this. The earthly world is filled with physical pain and emotional suffering. Humans seek material pleasures. I don't want any of that. I'd rather stay here in this dimension for a while longer, if I may?"

The third spiritual being interjected. "This is an opportunity and a privilege for you! Many look forward to this! You have nothing to fear. We'll watch over you always."

A sense of soothing peace swirled around and rested upon the three of them like a soft, warm blanket. The purity of silence prevailed until a response finally came from the lower right. "I understand that you plan to watch over me as I forge ahead into physical presence. However, when I arrive there, on earth in human form, I'll no longer understand. I won't actually know that you're here … or there. I'm simply not ready to leave the peace and serenity that I have here in this dimension."

The Almighty One was not accustomed to being challenged on this issue. There was profound silence during what seemed to be a power struggle between the three of them.

The being on the left said, "You will soon have an earthly name, and we will never leave you. We realize that you're feeling a sense of loss and sadness right now, but this is meant to be a time for rejoicing! Let's make a deal. We'll provide you with glimpses of ourselves during your physical journey. We'll watch over you, and you'll eventually learn and understand this throughout your earthly life. We are here for you always. This will become an important part of your human existence. We'll keep our promise. You have nothing to fear. And when you return to us after your physical journey, you'll be better equipped for the good works here. You must go now."

Fluffy white clouds and brilliant blue skies suddenly turned black. The lower being on the right was immediately conceived in earthly form, and the remaining two spiritual beings continued to watch over.

Chapter 1
Supreme Suppression

February 2016

Elizabeth Reed stepped from a steaming hot shower onto a warm, soft bath mat. Her feet were exhausted. She longed to sit down for a moment, relax, sip a glass of wine, and stare out the window at the peaceful blanket of snow that had gently fallen throughout the day. But there was no time for that. She had spent the last two days setting up for two different community events, including the formal charity gala that she and Nick would be attending that evening.

Nick Reed was Elizabeth's best friend and husband of twenty-three years. She peered through the bathroom doors at his tuxedo, which was hanging on a dresser knob. He could easily get dressed in five minutes flat, but she needed at least another half hour. And they were already a few minutes late. They would need to bundle up since the temperatures had fallen to record lows for eastern North Carolina that evening.

The sound of the television blasted from the bedroom. Elizabeth realized that she hadn't watched the news in the past few days, and it was an election year. News was changing daily, and she had probably missed something important. What Elizabeth heard next suddenly rocked her to the core. Today, the news was personal.

The television announcer proclaimed, "United States Senator Edward Johnson died suddenly during his sleep last night, and was found in his bed this morning. No foul play is suspected. It is believed that he died from natural causes."

Elizabeth's heart raced. The beeping of a text startled her from across the room. She walked over to read it and saw that it was from her longtime friend who now lived in California. *Senator Johnson is dead.* Molly had also left a voice mail, saying, "Turn on the news. Senator Johnson is dead. Unbelievable! Call me."

Elizabeth took a deep breath and called Molly.

"Hello, Elizabeth. Can you believe it? Senator Johnson is gone."

"This is shocking," Elizabeth gasped. "Senator Johnson's son and his friends have tried more than once to destroy me over the years. They've threatened my life repeatedly. Could Edward Johnson have known just enough about this mess to feel like my extended safety net? And if he was indeed ever a safety net, the safety net is gone."

After a moment of discussion, Elizabeth hung up the phone. She needed to hurry and get dressed for the gala. She needed to block this from her mind, at least for the night. She was partially responsible for running the gala since she served on the board of directors for the charity.

Elizabeth could handle the pressure. She had become very skilled at blocking trauma from her mind. She had been doing it quite well for the past thirty-three years.

Chapter 2
Spring Break, 1983

Thirty-Three Years Earlier

Elizabeth and her friends drove away from campus at the University of South Carolina on a sunny Friday afternoon, stayed one night in Daytona Beach, and drove several more hours into Fort Lauderdale. From that point forward, Elizabeth was stuck in a tiny motel room with peeling floral wallpaper and a very old bathroom, with seven other girls from her dorm. Some were good friends she had met the previous year. Others were acquaintances who lived on her hallway. Everyone knew one another, but some were closer than others. But at least they were all sharing the expense.

During the first few fun-filled days, they spent time on the beach and explored the area. As the week went on, tension of having eight people stuffed into one tiny motel room was growing. And money was tight. There was a vending machine in the back of the motel by the pool bar. Elizabeth had made ends meet by purchasing cheese and peanut butter crackers from the vending machine for several meals. She couldn't afford to spend money on drinks that week, and was often sober while others were not. Part of her entertainment had been the mere act of people watching, particularly drunk people.

On the second day of spring break, Elizabeth and her friends Rebecca and Lacey were selected to be judges in a well-attended belly flop contest. The contest was held at the pool of a popular nearby hotel. Each day, the large hotel hosted students from selected colleges for fun local events and contests.

On the afternoon of the belly flop contest, hundreds of people watched the contestants soar into the pool with arms and legs spread widely apart, only to land flat on their bellies! It appeared to be painful, but the person who splashed the most water, with the loudest *flop,* would be the champion.

Before the contest, a large young man walked over to Elizabeth and the other judges and quietly proclaimed, "Pick me as your winner—and you'll all enjoy free cocaine for the rest of the week!"

Elizabeth and the other judges were astounded. He walked away with a smile. The judges discussed what he had said and made their decision.

When the young man with the cocaine promises stepped onto the diving board, he soared high into the air with arms and legs spread before sailing down into the water with a superior-sounding *flop!* The crowd roared. Several other contestants had been as loud and splashed just as much water. The competition was close.

He gloated as he stepped out of the pool, awaiting his score. The judges smiled back at him. Elizabeth went first and gave him a score of one on a scale of one to five. He fumed. Each judge thereafter gave him low scores. He was infuriated.

The crowd was confused when another winner was awarded the grand prize of one hundred dollars. Some were angry at what they viewed as an unfair competition.

When the contest was over, the angry loser walked over to the judges and said, "You'll all pay for this!"

Elizabeth and the other judges quickly left the premises, but they weren't really concerned about him. He'd have to get over his loss and learn to play fair. None of the judges had ever considered being bribed with cocaine, which he had found out the hard way.

On their third morning in Fort Lauderdale, a new buzz was circulating about the next popular contest for the female spring breakers. Before the morning was over, Rebecca announced to

Elizabeth that she was planning to enter a wet T-shirt contest that afternoon. It would be easy money, and she encouraged Elizabeth to join her. However, as tight as money was, Elizabeth couldn't imagine standing on a stage with a room full of people staring at her breasts. It was inconceivable. She didn't even like to get dressed in front of the other girls in their motel room. She was modest and preferred going into the bathroom to change clothes. She never considered the nightmare of standing on stage under these circumstances.

A couple hours later, Elizabeth, Rebecca, and Lacey walked to the bar for the contest. Rebecca told everyone that she might reconsider, depending on who else was at the bar. She didn't want Sandy or the other girls knowing that she was planning to enter the contest.

On that stormy afternoon, all the bars were crowded. At this particular bar, all females received free drinks until the beginning of the contest. It was a genius idea to acquire more entries for the contest.

After Rebecca had consumed a couple of free drinks, the emcee called for all females who wanted to enter the wet T-shirt contest to please join him on stage. Rebecca was getting nervous and consumed her third drink in one big gulp. Only four girls were standing on the stage.

Lacey, Elizabeth, and Rebecca began laughing when they realized that Rebecca actually had small breasts. Should she reconsider? She was of American Indian descent with smooth, dark, flawless skin. She was tall and lean with dark curly hair. Her breast size didn't seem to matter. She would still be considered a welcome participant in this contest. But Rebecca was reconsidering.

The emcee announced that all contestants would receive a hundred dollars in cash simply for coming on stage to enter the contest! "See how easy this is?" he shouted out to the crowd.

With that announcement, Rebecca slammed her empty cup on the table and ran onto the stage, along with six or seven additional contestants. The emcee announced that he would accept no more contestants, and the contest was ready to begin. The winner would soon be chosen according to the loudest applause.

The emcee gave the contestants T-shirts and asked them to remove their bathing suit tops, shirts, and bras. They could wear only the T-shirts. They weren't allowed to leave the stage to do this. They could turn their backs to the crowd if they wanted, but they were not allowed to leave the stage while changing.

Two of the girls immediately walked off stage and disqualified themselves. They couldn't follow through with it. Elizabeth knew that she could have never participated in this contest.

Within seconds, water began sprinkling heavily from above the stage and onto the contestants. Black mascara dripped down their cheeks. Their hair was drenched and falling into their faces. Their breasts were glowing through the wet T-shirts. It appeared humiliating, and Elizabeth was growing more and more horrified.

A young man walked across the stage with a hose and squirted them from head to toe. Each contestant was taken aback by the pressure of the water.

"These girls are earning their cash!" the emcee proclaimed. "We don't give away money that easily!" He played "Super Freak" and ordered the contestants to dance.

Elizabeth and Lacey were beginning to feel sick about this whole ordeal. Rebecca was dancing with all eyes upon her. When the time finally came for applause, Rebecca received the least applause.

"That's okay," the emcee announced. "That was only a trial round! You girls need to have another shot!" At that moment, a bartender walked onto the stage and handed each contestant a shot of liquor. "It's getting hot in here! Have a drink!"

The girls gulped the liquor.

"Now you girls have a chance to double your money!" the emcee announced. "Remove your T-shirt for another hundred dollars!"

The wet T-shirt contest was transforming into a striptease show, but Rebecca didn't think twice. She was the first contestant to remove her T-shirt and slam it to the floor.

Elizabeth shrieked and the crowd roared.

The contestant who had already received the most applause didn't remove her T-shirt, but all the others did.

The emcee played a new song and ordered them all to dance. He asked the audience to watch closely and vote for their favorite stripper. Elizabeth looked around the room and noticed that most of the guys were staring intently; the girls were covering their faces with disgust and shame. She was growing more and more embarrassed for Rebecca.

A young man standing near Elizabeth and the others asked, "Didn't one of those girls come here with you?"

Lacey nodded. "We didn't realize she was capable of this." They looked at each other and knew they didn't want to be associated with that activity. The girls on stage were being transformed into objects of pleasure.

During the final round of voting, Rebecca received more applause than the first time, but she didn't win the overall competition. However, removing her shirt had certainly helped her gain more applause, and it had also helped her win more money. When the contest was over, she picked up her dry shirt and put it back on. Upon returning to Lacey and Elizabeth, she proclaimed with a big bright smile, "That was definitely worth two hundred dollars, but don't you dare tell anyone outside of this room what just happened in here!"

Chapter 3
The Meeting

With three nights still remaining of her trip in Fort Lauderdale, Elizabeth returned to her motel after enjoying a much-needed all-you-can-eat seafood buffet with Danielle, Rebecca, and Sue. Their room was filled with people.

Elizabeth immediately noticed Chad across the room. He was sitting on a chair next to one of the beds and was listening to music with two more unfamiliar men. She didn't recognize any of them, but she immediately noticed Chad's bright smile and big brown eyes. She was smitten at the sight of him. She had never been much of a flirt, but the sight of him took her breath away.

Chad and his friends had returned to Elizabeth's room after happy hour to listen to music with Sandy. Elizabeth sat down on the edge of the bed with her back to Chad and took a deep breath as Sandy entertained everyone. Sandy danced and shouted the words to "Let's Groove Tonight" by Earth, Wind & Fire. She had already had a few drinks and tried to get Elizabeth to dance and sing with her. Elizabeth, who was sober, declined. She sat at the edge of the bed, swayed her shoulders, and softly sang along. Elizabeth was gradually growing more comfortable.

The music stopped. Chad moved over to sit next to Elizabeth and asked where she was from.

"South Carolina" she replied softly with a smile.

"Hey, are you from Charleston?" he asked with enthusiasm. "I visited there a few years ago. It's incredibly beautiful and historic."

"Nope, I'm from a small town in the northern part of the state. How about you? You sound like you're from the North."

"Boston area," he replied.

Chad introduced Elizabeth to Luke and Steve. Luke was tall and lanky with strawberry-blonde hair and freckles. Steve had dark skin, dark hair, and a stern look. Chad asked if everyone wanted to go to a dance club. Everyone in the room agreed, and they began walking.

Chad walked next to Elizabeth and asked if she went to the University of South Carolina with Sandy and Rebecca.

She replied, "Yes. How about you? Where do you go to school?"

"Have you ever heard of Boston College?" Chad asked.

"Of course I've heard of Boston College!" Elizabeth concluded that he was a student at Boston College.

"Not many people around here seem to know about it. They all know about Boston University, but not Boston College. Are you sure you're not getting the two confused?" he elaborated.

"Of course I'm sure. I know the difference." Elizabeth recalled a recent conversation with her dad about Doug Flutie, an outstanding football player from Boston College. It seemed that the only meaningful conversations she ever had with her dad were about football. This caused particular conversations to stand out in her mind. During their recent discussion about Doug Flutie, they had also discussed the size of Boston College.

Elizabeth didn't appreciate the fact that Chad doubted her knowledge of the difference between Boston College and Boston University. She continued, "Not only have I heard of Boston College, but I can tell you that there are about five thousand students who attend that school." Her smile widened.

Chad looked at her unknowingly before turning to Luke. "Is she right about that? How many students attend Boston College?"

Luke appeared to do some calculations in his head, adding up the number of freshman, sophomores, juniors, and seniors. "Yes, there are about five thousand total students. She's right." Luke nodded.

"Okay, so you're right about that. Good guess!" Chad said with a sly smile.

"That wasn't a guess."

"Okay. What state is Boston College in?" Chad asked.

"You can't be serious. Boston is in Massachusetts. Good grief."

Chad continued to quiz Elizabeth about her knowledge of the United States and its history as they strolled down the sidewalk.

Elizabeth was growing more and more smitten with his silly charm. History wasn't her favorite subject, but she enjoyed watching Chad and his fascination with it. Chad had an uncanny ability to make United States history feel fun and exciting.

Elizabeth mentioned that Florida seemed to have a more Northern culture, even though it was geographically the most southern state. She told him that she had ordered tea in the restaurant earlier that evening. At first, the waiter had brought hot tea, which would never happen in South Carolina. After finally bringing iced tea, the restaurant charged her for every refill. She was accustomed to tea refills being complimentary back in South Carolina. She had spent far more money than expected for dinner because of the extra charges for numerous tea refills. When Chad offered to buy her a Long Island iced tea to make up for her loss, she accepted but immediately felt guilty. She was relieved when he proclaimed, "Why don't we have our own little Boston Tea Party? Let's make a deal. I'll buy you a Long Island iced tea, but you have to promise not to throw it in the ocean!"

As they entered the bar, Chad continued, "When all these college students come down here and invade these local businesses, they either love us or hate us." He stopped at the bar before turning toward her. "And there's a fine line between love and hate, my dear." He playfully tapped the tip of her nose while using his other hand to gracefully slip a Long Island iced tea through her fingers.

Elizabeth smiled and thanked him.

They danced together through the evening, including a few slow dances. Elizabeth's admiration was growing stronger. She learned that Chad worked part time as a waiter and bellman at an affluent hotel in Boston. He was a speed-reader and carried an impressive course load with a master plan to finish both undergraduate and medical school within five years. He wanted to get married one day and have as many children as possible. She was impressed that his goals were already well-defined.

"Why don't we take a walk outside where it's quiet?" Chad shouted. "We can talk and actually hear what we're saying to one another."

Elizabeth agreed.

"What's your favorite type of music?" Chad asked.

"I like all types of music…except for heavy metal."

"But what's your favorite? What do you listen to when you're at home?"

"I listen to Earth, Wind & Fire and the Jackson Five's early songs. I like Boston too. That was my first concert. What do you think about them?"

"Actually, I prefer the Boston Pops. Have you heard of them?"

"No."

"They're a symphony orchestra. Do you like that type of music?"

"I don't listen to it very much, but I like it."

"Do you like Frank Sinatra?" he asked.

"Of course I love Frank Sinatra. Doesn't everybody?" Elizabeth replied.

"These clowns I'm with don't like to listen to him. You and I just found common ground. What are some of your favorite Frank Sinatra songs?"

Elizabeth couldn't recall a time when anyone had ever asked her so many specific questions about her likes and dislikes. She couldn't recall a time when anyone took so much interest in her at all. She had never been comfortable talking about herself in detail. "I attempted to play many Frank Sinatra songs on the piano in my younger years. Even though I loved his music, I never really excelled at playing piano. I like 'Strangers In the Night,'" she laughed.

They continued to talk about their likes and dislikes. Elizabeth loved animals. Chad had never had pets of any kind, while Elizabeth had owned dogs, cats, fish, birds, an alligator, ducks, guinea pigs, and a monkey. She shared some of her favorite pet stories with Chad. He laughed, but he couldn't seem to relate.

"When I went down to South Carolina, we attended the Spoleto Arts Festival in Charleston. Did you ever attend that?" Chad asked.

"No, I've never attended it. I haven't spent much time down in Charleston at all. How did you like it?"

"You live that close to the Spoleto Festival, and you've never attended? You need to go one year."

"You're right. I've heard it's spectacular."

Elizabeth was beginning to feel a gap between them. Not to mention, Chad was confident and secure about his future. Elizabeth was uncertain about her future. She had already changed majors once, and she wasn't sure if she was making the right decisions.

Chad informed Elizabeth that he only had tonight and tomorrow night remaining for his time in Fort Lauderdale. After that, he was flying back into Boston, and then he would quickly re-pack for a long weekend trip to Hawaii. His dad was at a convention, and would be receiving an award there. Chad planned to attend the ceremony.

Chad was jet-setting nationwide, and she had never flown on a plane. She had traveled to many areas throughout the United States, but only by car. She suddenly felt very unglamorous.

"Have you ever been up around New England, where I live?" Chad asked.

Elizabeth told him about a family trip to Manhattan and New England. She avoided telling him that they had traveled in a station wagon. She avoided telling him that she and her brother had been crammed into the back hatch of a station wagon for fourteen hours each way. Another family of three accompanied them, and they required the entire backseat. Seven people had traveled to the 1976 bicentennial celebration. She wanted to change the subject as quickly as possible.

Chad asked her to walk with him down the beach. Finally, he gazed into her pale green eyes, took her into his arms, and kissed her gently. It felt magical to Elizabeth. They walked and talked and kissed, and eventually the kisses became more passionate.

"I want to do something. Bear with me." He grabbed her hand and led her up to his room on the third floor of their motel.

Elizabeth's heart was fluttering. She waited outside. His friends were inside watching television. Chad told them to make dinner plans elsewhere without him. He wanted to spend a little more time with Elizabeth. He mentioned that he needed to grab a few items from the room, before leaving with two coolers, a beach towel, and a blanket. "I'll bring it all back," he promised as he shut the door.

Elizabeth and Chad returned to the beach. He created a tent of sorts. He tied and draped the blanket across the top of the two coolers and put the beach towel on the sand between the coolers. They crawled inside of the tent and kissed more passionately. Chad untied the strings of her dress at her shoulders, loosening the top, and pulled it down to her waist. He stared deeply into her eyes and stroked her long blonde hair.

Elizabeth arched her back as he unhooked her strapless bra, exposing her breasts. She pulled his shirt over his head, and they held their warm bodies close, intimately exploring each other. Her dress length was below the knee, but Chad gently pulled it toward her waist, caressing her thighs along the way.

Elizabeth explored his strong arms and muscular chest. His fingers moved from her breasts, then slowly downward, and Elizabeth suddenly stopped him. "I'm really sorry. You're amazing, but we need to slow down. We've barely known each other two hours." As much as she was enjoying their newfound chemistry, things couldn't go any further that night. She apologized for leading him along this far.

Chad was gracious and understanding.

They stayed hidden for a little while longer before finding their way back into the outside world. Elizabeth helped him take down the faux tent items and carry them back toward the motel.

"Why don't we see what tomorrow holds?" he asked. A cool breeze wisped softly around them.

Elizabeth shivered.

"You can't seriously be cold! It's snowing back home where I live."

"It's been much warmer than this lately … back home where I live," she answered.

"Do you work back home? Or do you just go to school?"

"I'm not working right now. I worked as a lifeguard for the last two summers, but I haven't worked yet this year. I don't have a car at school, but I need to find something part-time when I get back—with or without a car."

"You worked as a lifeguard? That's pretty cool. Where?"

"At a small pool in my hometown. It's really just a babysitting job. And we're the ones who keep the pools clean."

"Where have you been all week?"

"I've been right here all week. How about you?"

"Me too. How did I miss seeing you all week? I've seen Sandy and Rebecca every day at happy hour."

"Oh, I haven't been going to happy hour. We have eight girls staying in our room, and that's my afternoon shower time. We have a schedule."

"Would you like to have dinner with me tomorrow night? Do you like Italian food?"

"Oh, how sweet. Of course. I'd love to do that. That sounds nice."

"Can you believe there's a five-star restaurant on this strip? I wonder what kind of business they have around here. Anyway, I love Italian. I've wanted to go there all week, and I'd love to take you there."

"I'd love to go to dinner with you tomorrow night." Elizabeth was thrilled that Chad wanted to spend more time with her.

They stood at her door before saying good night. Chad gasped, "Your waist is tiny. I can fit both my hands all the way around it. Wow."

"No, my waist is not tiny. You just have big hands."

"Well, you know what they say about guys with big hands, don't you?"

She laughed. "Yes, it means that you also have big … feet."

"Feet? No, that's not what they say. Guess again."

She knew what he wanted her to say, but she had no intention of saying it. "Okay. Does it mean that you also have big eyes? You do have big beautiful eyes, my dear."

"No, that's not what it means either. But thank you. Guess again."

"Big smile? You have a big, beautiful smile."

"Nope."

"Okay, I give up. You'll just have to tell me what it means."

They kissed gently and said good night. She opened the door and stepped inside.

Closing the door, he softly whispered, "Big cock."

She smiled and said, "Good night."

Good grief. I feel like such a prude. I'm not a prude. I could have said that word! Of course I could have said that word. Thousands of people shout that word at sporting events. Go Cocks! She laughed to herself. Elizabeth had been so focused on not saying the word *penis* aloud that she never considered her own school's mascot. The South Carolina Gamecocks were known as the Cocks. She'd been around the word in such a different context over the years that it never occurred to her to say it. She should have had fun with it, she thought, before falling asleep with a big smile.

Chapter 4
The Morning After

"Everybody up," Sue shouted, clapping her hands as she scurried around the room. "We need to be at Jim's house in less than an hour for our boat ride!"

Jim was a friend who lived in their dorm at South Carolina. His parents lived in Fort Lauderdale and owned a large fishing boat. Jim had invited all of them over for a boat outing with his family. Elizabeth had forgotten to mention it to Chad. She had become so enthralled with him the night before that she never considered it.

"How long will we be gone?" Elizabeth asked.

"You don't have to go if you don't want to go," Sue responded.

"I want to go, but Chad asked me out to dinner tonight. Will we be back in time for that?"

Sandy answered, "We can probably ask Chad to come along with us. How about that?"

"I don't know. That feels presumptuous," Elizabeth muttered. "I just met him last night."

Sue replied, "We should be back after lunch. We're just going out for a couple of hours. Jim's dad made lunch for us too."

Elizabeth nodded. "Okay. We can leave a note on the door. Chad was so nice last night. I hate to rush off and be gone all morning without saying a word. And this is his last day here. He's leaving tomorrow."

Elizabeth wrote a note and taped it to the door.

To Chad and everyone else,

We're out on a boat ride all morning. We'll return after lunch.

—The Girls from Room #3.

They rushed to get ready before driving to Jim's house.

Jim's father greeted them with juice and muffins. Everyone introduced themselves before getting on the boat. It was a beautiful, warm day with sunny skies and warm sunshine, but the water was choppy, which caused the boat to rock up and down continuously.

It didn't take long for Elizabeth to start feeling seasick.

She stared straight ahead and watched the front of the boat bounce up and down on the turbulent waves. She tried to think of something pleasant, such as Chad with his big smile, but her stomach was growing weaker. Meeting Chad had been the highlight of her week, but she had scurried away early instead of spending time with him. She was beginning to feel nauseous. "Can you please tell me where the bathroom is?"

Jim and his dad apologized for the conditions and pointed her toward a bathroom down below. "There's a place to lie down too. That might help. You can't see or feel the turbulence as much down there either. We're really sorry."

"No need to apologize. Thank you for having us. I didn't expect this to happen. I'm sorry for raining on everyone's parade!" Elizabeth ran downstairs and vomited violently into the toilet. Every time she tried to hold up her head, she felt worse.

Jim showed her the bed in the next room and brought a wet towel for her head. For the next two hours, she went back and forth from the bed to the toilet. By the time they returned to land, Elizabeth was so weak that she couldn't eat lunch. She could barely stand as she walked to the car and waited in the backseat for everyone to eat lunch. A carbonated soda helped her feel slightly better by the time they returned to the motel.

As soon as Elizabeth stepped out of the car, she saw Chad and his friends.

"Thanks for leaving me here all alone this morning," Chad immediately teased with a pouted face.

"I'm sorry. I missed you. Didn't you notice that we specifically put your name on the note?" Elizabeth replied.

"Yes, I noticed. Thank you for thinking of me. It would have been much nicer if I could have actually gone along with you instead," Chad replied with a wink.

Elizabeth was taken aback. "Oh. We should have asked you to come along. But you wouldn't have seen me anyway. I had to go down below. I've been seasick this whole time. It was very embarrassing."

"I'm teasing, but I'm sorry that happened. I could have gone along to help take care of you," Chad whispered softly.

"That's sweet, but it was really very embarrassing. In fact, I'm a mess right now. I need to lie down for a little while longer. Please give me a few minutes to try to shake this." Elizabeth went to her room to lie down. The bed felt soft and inviting. Before she fell asleep, she thought about how nice it was to meet someone like Chad.

A short while later, several loud knocks caused Elizabeth to sit up and scurry to the door. When she opened it, Chad was standing in front of her. She felt pale, weak, and tired.

"This is my last full day here," he said. "The sunshine will make you feel much better than this tiny room, don't you think?"

Elizabeth wanted nothing more than to please him, but she knew it would be a tall task to do so while she felt physically ill. She told herself that she could rally for Chad. He was the best thing that had happened to her all week. "Can't you see that I'm a mess?"

"You look fine, really."

"Fine?" She laughed.

"You look better than fine. I want you to come upstairs with me to my room. I have something to show you."

A shiver rumbled through Elizabeth's body.

"What was that? Do I frighten you?" Chad reached toward her and gently massaged her shoulders.

"No. Of course you don't frighten me. I just need to brush my teeth and comb my hair." She went into the bathroom and straightened herself up before they walked up to his room.

When Chad opened the door, Eric Johnson stepped out of the bathroom. He was brushing his teeth. "Hey! Can't you give some kind of warning before bringing a girl in here? I could have been walking around naked!"

Chad introduced Elizabeth to Eric, who had not gone with them to the bar the night before. Eric greeted them briefly before stepping back into the bathroom.

Luke Madison was sitting on the bed watching television.

Chad grabbed a menu from the dresser and handed it to Elizabeth. "I walked down to that five-star restaurant this morning and made reservations for two. They gave me this menu. Take a look."

Eric stepped out of the bathroom. Elizabeth noticed that Luke and Eric were rolling their eyes at each other, but she didn't acknowledge them. *Just what I need—another reason to feel uncomfortable.*

"So what are you thinking about ordering?" Chad asked.

Elizabeth turned the pages of the extensive menu. Her stomach still wasn't quite right. Reading through descriptions of rich food didn't help, but she wanted to show her appreciation for his generosity. "Actually, I've never heard of most of the items on the menu."

Luke and Eric rolled their eyes at each other again.

Chad saw them this time, but didn't waiver. "Would you please allow me to make a few choice recommendations for you, madam?" He bowed, slipped the menu from her hand, and stepped back.

"That would be delightful. Thank you, sir," she replied with a smile.

"I'd like to recommend the Calamari Alla Griglia as an appetizer. It's spectacular. And for the main course, the Papperdelle con Granchio. I had a dish similar to this in Manhattan a few weeks ago, and it was quite delightful. And to complement your palate, I'll recommend the Chateau Latour wine with its rich cherry fruit layered between countless aromas bundled into a very powerful but classy package."

"That sounds fabulous. I'll take your recommendation," Elizabeth replied.

Chad asked Luke and Eric to step into the bathroom for a second. "I want to ask Elizabeth a personal question."

Luke and Eric didn't seem thrilled with the idea of being ordered around in their tiny living space, but they reluctantly obliged. In that moment, Elizabeth understood that she was quickly becoming an object of inconvenience for Chad's friends.

Chad grabbed her shoulder and led her away from the bathroom. He said softly, "I have a question for you."

Elizabeth realized exactly why she wanted to rally for Chad. She understood why she had followed him up to his motel room again this morning—in spite of her queasy stomach and petty insecurities. He possessed the uncanny ability to look through her eyes and deeply into her soul. There was a familiarity with him; it was almost as if she'd known him before. She was mesmerized by his smile and worldly charm. Her knees weakened, and she felt short of breath. "Ask me anything," she whispered. Butterflies were taking flight across her already churning stomach. She couldn't imagine what he was about to ask.

"Can we finish what we started last night?"

"What do you mean?"

"You know what I mean—what we were doing last night on the beach."

His question caught her off guard, causing the butterflies in her stomach to stop flying. She was riding an emotional roller coaster. She didn't think before loudly proclaiming, "That conversation belongs in the red-light district!"

Luke and Eric stepped out from the bathroom with widened eyes.

Chad waved them both away and turned to Elizabeth. "Let's step outside." They stepped out onto the breezeway. "Are you feeling okay?"

"No, actually, I'm not. Chad, you've been pushing me all morning. I was really sick on that boat this morning. I'm trying to rally for you, but I didn't expect you to ask me that question, especially in front of those guys."

"Their names are Luke and Eric."

"I didn't expect for you to ask me that question in front of Luke and Eric."

"Okay, but your response was insulting. I offered to take you to a five-star restaurant, and you responded like I was some sort of lowlife. Quite frankly, you embarrassed me in front of Luke and Eric."

"That wasn't my intention at all. You're so adorable. I'm really sorry if I offended you."

"Okay. Do you want to meet me out on the beach in a few minutes?"

"Yes. That sounds great. I'll see you in a few." As Elizabeth walked back toward her room, she wondered why Luke, Eric, and Chad had been so astonished at her comment about the red-light district. They had looks of horror on their faces. Chad was terribly offended.

Elizabeth didn't realize that, at age nineteen, she didn't know the meaning of the term. In fact, she simply believed that she had told Chad to stop the conversation because she didn't like the direction it was going. She thought that she had simply asked him to change the subject. A red light means to stop.

She recalled an earlier conversation between two of her high school friends. One of them had said, "That conversation belongs in the red-light district." Everyone around them concluded that they should change the subject. Therefore, Elizabeth concluded this was a slang expression meaning to stop the conversation and change its direction. Elizabeth was too naïve and sheltered to understand that a red-light district was actually a term for areas of town where prostitutes solicit business.

***

Chad, Luke, Eric, and Steve had all lived in and around big cities. They all knew the real definition of a red light district —and none of them liked it.

Chad stepped back into his motel room with Luke and Eric. Steve came in from the beach a moment later and asked, "I just saw Elizabeth walking back to her room. Was she up here just now?"

"Yep," Luke answered. "We don't know what to think about any of this. And we certainly can't figure her out."

Chad reluctantly confessed, "I'm having second thoughts about taking Elizabeth to dinner."

Steve asked, "Why would you do that anyway? You're about to get engaged to Jan, aren't you?"

Chapter 5
The Betrayals

Eric stepped toward Chad and said, "This is supposed to be a guy's trip. We thought you were in love with Jan. What exactly is going on here?"

"I am in love with Jan ... or at least I think I am," Chad answered. "I need to be sure. What's wrong with that? I'm not married yet. Heck, I'm not even engaged yet. That's a huge lifelong decision."

"Well, we can certainly help you make your decision. You don't need Elizabeth. We're going to see plenty of girls tonight at that strip club. It's your last night here. Come on! We came down here to celebrate your engagement!"

"Is that really the only reason we came down here?" Chad asked. "My dad told me that if I came down here and met someone, to please take her out and do a little more self-discovery before making such a huge decision. I've only known Jan for a few months."

Chad had met Luke, Steve and Eric during various points throughout his life. And now, they all attended different elite universities. Until this trip, they hadn't seen each other since Christmas.

"This could be our last night together as single men," Luke exclaimed. "The next time we're together, it could be for your wedding, Chad. We were under the impression that this trip would be your bachelor party!"

A few weeks before the trip, Chad had called each of them to tell them about Jan. He had met her when she came to his family home in Massachusetts to help take care of his severely autistic sister. Jan had been appointed to help their family for a few weeks as part of a school assignment.

Prior to coming to Fort Lauderdale, Chad had told his friends that he was considering marriage. However, he had never considered this trip a bachelor party. When he arrived, they wouldn't allow him to help pay for the motel room.

Chad's friends refused to share their time with Elizabeth on this trip. One way for them to put a stop to it was by persuading Chad to go to the strip club on their last night in Fort Lauderdale. They had been looking forward to it all week. Luke, Eric, and Steve convinced Chad that going to the strip club tonight was not a subject for negotiation. He needed to change his plans with Elizabeth.

Chad's friends were important to him. Eric was from a powerful political family. His father was a personal friend to President Ronald Reagan. Eric planned to become a lawyer and was proud of his family's growing prominence and power.

Luke was a historian and wanted to get involved in politics. He was class president at an elite university, yet he was generally quiet and reserved. Steve was also a historian who aspired to teach history or work in a museum.

All four young men deeply cared about America and felt that its future was fragile. They were excited about Ronald Reagan's policies and vision, and they knew he was leading the country in a positive new direction, which was desperately needed following the Jimmy Carter administration. They were strongly opposed to any person who could possibly jeopardize the fate of America.

"Let's go down to the beach," Steve urged.

They gathered sunscreen, towels, and coolers and walked down to the beach. Chad was unsure how he could cancel his plans with Elizabeth without seriously offending her. He had also befriended Rebecca and Sandy. If he canceled his plans with Elizabeth, he would probably need to answer to them too.

Upon arrival at the beach, Chad sat on his towel and pondered his next move. Within moments, Elizabeth was standing over him. He was stunned by what he saw. He recognized her bathing suit from earlier in the week - before he had actually met her!

He sat up straight. "Elizabeth, do you remember me?"

"Excuse me? Is this a trick question? Of course I remember you."

"Elizabeth, I'm referring to what happened to us earlier this week. You and I were both standing out in the water. You sure do look different in that bathing suit. This is unbelievable!" He laughed. "You and I didn't put this together last night!" He shook his head. "And you still haven't put it together, have you?" He looked deeply into her eyes.

Earlier during the week, Chad and his friends had noticed Elizabeth on the beach. They had watched her play volleyball. Soon thereafter, when Chad was standing next to her in the water, a wave came along and knocked down the bottom of her suit to her knees. She immediately pulled up her bathing suit to cover herself, but Chad had already seen everything. It happened quickly, but he had been deeply offended. He didn't see any humor in it, and humiliated Elizabeth in front everyone. He accused her of wearing a cheap bathing suit.

"Don't you remember our encounter earlier this week? Do you remember what happened to that bathing suit out there in the water? I was standing right next to you."

Elizabeth's eyes widened. "Oh...that was you. That was horrible. A wave came along, and you overreacted. I didn't cause that to happen."

"It doesn't matter. I hate that bathing suit! You worked as a lifeguard wearing a bathing suit like that?"

Chad decided that he could use it as an opportunity to go their separate ways. "As you can see, we've known each other for less than twenty-four hours, but we already have baggage. We need to move on. I need to spend my last night down here with my friends. I came down here to be with them, and I don't want to let them down. I'm sorry I led you on, but we need to cancel our dinner plans."

Elizabeth was clearly disappointed, hurt, and embarrassed. "Well, it was nice knowing you, Chad. Enjoy the rest of your trip," she said as she waved to him and walked quietly across the loud and crowded beach. She sat next to Sandy and turned in the opposite direction. A few teardrops trickled down her face, but she quickly wiped them away.

As she wiped away another tear, Sandy yelled, "Come on! Let's play some more volleyball!" Elizabeth grabbed her shorts and a T-shirt and covered her bathing suit. She jumped up and joined the game. Most of the other players were from the University of South Carolina.

Meanwhile, Chad was beginning to have regrets about sending Elizabeth away so quickly. He sat up and watched her play. He was physically attracted to her, and he enjoyed listening to her southern accent. He had already made a decision about his future, and Elizabeth was not in it. *Or was she?* He admired her resilience. She was laughing and enjoying herself with Sandy and the others.

Chad had spent much more time with Sandy and Rebecca than he had with Elizabeth. He had especially enjoyed spending time with them at happy hour every afternoon. They were fun, but he was much more physically attracted to Elizabeth. When the volleyball match ended, he decided that he wasn't ready to give up on her yet. Without thinking about how he might handle this with Luke, Steve, and Eric, he walked over and apologized. He asked her if she would sit with him for a while.

***

Elizabeth felt uneasy. She had already concluded that Luke, Steve and Eric didn't want to share their time with Chad on this trip. But she picked up her towel anyway and sat with them.

"Elizabeth, are you a Republican or a Democrat?" Eric immediately asked.

"I really don't know," Elizabeth replied. She had no interest in politics.

"She's an Independent," Chad replied.

"Well, do you happen to know if Ronald Reagan is a Republican or a Democrat?" Eric asked.

"I think he's a Republican," Elizabeth answered.

Eric sneered and said, "Well, at least she knew that much." He turned to Elizabeth again. "Thank God we got rid of that southern president, Jimmy Carter! What a disaster that was!"

Elizabeth was the only southerner in the conversation. All four of them glared at her.

"Is that comment supposed to offend me as a southerner?" she asked. "I didn't vote for him."

"Of course you didn't vote for him. You weren't old enough to vote back then," Eric sneered.

Elizabeth didn't allow them to bother her with their rudeness. "Have you all been enjoying your week down here?"

Steve answered, "We've been sitting and staring and sitting and staring for five days in a row. What kind of week do you think we're having? We're bored."

"Well, I'm sure that you've managed to have at least one or two pleasant conversations over the past five days, right? Why just sit here and stare?"

"Okay, I deserved that."

"And you're welcome to play volleyball with us whenever you'd like. We're having fun."

"Is that all you've been doing all week, playing volleyball?" Eric asked.

"Not exactly," Elizabeth answered. "There have been some interesting events along the strip this week."

"The what?" Luke gasped.

Eric replied to Luke, "The *strip*. That's what they call that street with the bars and restaurants." He pointed toward the street.

"Oh, I see," Luke replied.

Elizabeth stared at them for a moment before telling them about her experience as a judge in the belly flop contest. She told them about the contestant who should have won and how he tried to bribe them. "The irony is that he would have won that contest if he hadn't tried to bribe us with drugs in the first place."

"Oh my God!" Eric replied. "That guy could still come after you now, don't you think?"

"Oh, I'm not worried about him. That was days ago. He should have known better than to do that. But we did get out of there in a hurry. We left as soon as the contest was over!"

Eric mumbled, "She's naive."

Chad appeared uncomfortable. "Can you walk with me up to the pool for a few minutes? I need to walk around and stretch my legs," he asked.

Elizabeth stood up. They walked across the street. Chad told Elizabeth that he needed to use the restroom, and walked into the pool bar.

She went to her motel room to freshen up.

A few moments later, when she stepped out of her motel room, Chad was standing with Sandy and Rebecca and a couple of other people she didn't recognize. They were all standing next to the pool bar. Elizabeth walked up behind Chad, looked across at Sandy and Rebecca and smiled at them.

"Elizabeth! Why did you do that?" Rebecca and Sandy asked. Their eyes widened.

"Do what?" Elizabeth asked. She looked around at the others.

"That smile! What was that all about?" Sandy asked.

"I smiled at you to say hello. That's all. Are you kidding me?" Elizabeth replied.

"You were mocking Chad's sister!" Sandy shrieked.

"Whoa! I don't know anything about Chad's sister! I smiled at both of you when I walked up. I was acknowledging you to say hello. What on earth is wrong with you, Sandy?"

"It was the way you smiled. And you smiled as soon as we mentioned Chad's sister. You looked exactly like you were mocking a mentally challenged person," Sandy explained. "I helped volunteer with Special Olympics last summer. That's how they smile—with really big, wide smiles. And people make fun of them by doing that!"

Elizabeth was stunned. "Well, maybe people do make fun of them by doing that, but I am not one of those people. You should know me better than that!"

Chad turned around. "How long have you been standing here?"

"I've only been standing here for a few seconds. I didn't hear what you were talking about. This is absolutely crazy. I don't know anything about your sister, Chad."

"You didn't hear anything we said?" Chad asked.

"No!"

Rebecca interjected, "Elizabeth, you were standing there long enough to hear what we said. We mentioned Chad's sister, and you smiled. Surely you know about Chad's sister."

"Chad hasn't mentioned his sister to me. Why are you allowing this to continue? You're way out of line—both of you! I would never mock anybody like that. This is wrong!" She looked at Chad in anguish.

"I'll handle this." Chad pulled Elizabeth away from them to speak to her privately. "Why would they say that about you? What exactly have you done that would make them believe you'd do that? I'm curious."

"I don't know, Chad. It's inexplicable. Tell me about your sister."

"She has a severe case of autism. She rarely speaks and gets around only in a wheelchair."

Elizabeth appeared sympathetic.

"See, that's what I don't like. I don't like people to feel sorry for me because of this. We have plenty of help with her at home. I told Sandy and Rebecca about her earlier this week. They assumed that you knew too."

"You should have told me."

"I don't usually tell people as soon as I meet them. I don't want to be defined by my sister or by any of my family members. There are plenty of ignorant people in this world who do mock my sister. It makes me really angry when people do that. Do you understand?"

"Yes, of course. I'm sorry."

"Stop apologizing. I don't believe you meant any harm, but I am a bit curious now. Have you had any problems with Sandy and Rebecca this week? Why would they say that about you?"

"I've had no problems with them. I've been with them all morning, and everything's been fine. I can't speak about what's happening inside of their heads. I can only tell you what's happening inside of my own head."

"Some people spend their entire careers trying to figure out what's happening inside of other people's heads," Chad quipped

Elizabeth was beginning to feel sick again. She adored Chad. She had little tolerance for idle gossip, but this false accusation was overwhelming. Didn't they know she could never mock any mentally handicapped person, especially Chad's sister? Didn't they understand how much she liked Chad? Elizabeth felt as though she was becoming a mental punching bag.

Chad tried to help her understand. "Sandy evidently thought this because of your untimely smile. She's volunteered with Special Olympics and understands the dynamics. Rebecca seems pretty respectable. You need to figure out why they'd both say this about you. If their perception is severely wrong, you have serious damage control that you need to handle."

"I need to be alone for a few minutes." Elizabeth went to her room to think. She felt like a target—as if she couldn't do anything right. She was afraid to speak or move with other people around.

Rebecca was a part-time student who was struggling to pass the only two classes she was taking. She was more than likely feeling very insecure. Rebecca often experimented with drugs, which was why Elizabeth almost didn't go on the trip in the first place. Elizabeth had been concerned about spending time away from home around Rebecca's continuous bad habits; and she had been stunned to see her enter the wet T-shirt contest with such enthusiasm.

Rebecca had managed to keep the wet T-shirt contest a secret from almost everyone, which was incredible. Hundreds of people had been watching the contest that afternoon, but Sandy still didn't know about it. Chad had referred to Rebecca as respectable. If Elizabeth tried to tell Chad what she knew about Rebecca, it would seem like revenge or petty gossip—and she had no tolerance for either. She didn't want to fight fire with fire. She wasn't vengeful, and she had done nothing wrong when she smiled. She simply smiled to say hello—and nothing more—but evidently she smiled at the wrong time. She closed her eyes and prayed for peace, and for the truth to be known. She prayed that Chad would see what was in her heart as opposed to what was being said about her.

Elizabeth wished she could hide until it was time to go home, but Chad seemed like a sensible person; surely he could figure this out. She considered him a bright ray of sunshine. He was charming, sensible, humorous, and kind most of the time. His friends, however, were not as kind.

Everyone else had found their individual comfort zones in the last few days. Lacey was from New York, and she was spending most of her time with a group of high school friends who were staying in their same motel.

Sandy and Rebecca had become inseparable after the wet T-shirt contest—except for when Rebecca was sleeping around. Sandy still didn't know that Rebecca had entered the wet-T-shirt contest.

Danielle's boyfriend, George, was staying in a hotel down the street, and she was spending most of her time with him.

Molly had left town because she couldn't handle the chaos anymore. She called her parents' friends in West Palm Beach, and they picked her up. She stayed at their house for a few days.

Sue and Victoria spent most of their time at a different hotel with different groups of friends. Victoria was in a sorority, and her sorority sisters were staying down the street.

With eight girls in one room, they all needed personal space. The only comfort zone Elizabeth had found in the past twenty-four hours was Chad. She trusted him, but she also felt very alone. She sat alone in her quiet room and prayed for peace.

❊❊❊

Meanwhile, Chad walked toward the beach. He overheard two male students from the University of South Carolina discussing the wet T-shirt contest. He recognized them from the earlier volleyball match.

"She was in that crazy wet T-shirt contest earlier this week," one of them said. "Then she jumped right in the sack with a couple of different guys. I think she's messed up on drugs right now. Everybody thinks she's a full-time student, but she's only taking a couple of classes—and she never goes to either one. She's flunking out of school. It's sad. What a mess!"

Chad stormed past them in a rage. The two young men had never said her name, but Chad was certain they had been talking about Elizabeth. Who else could it be? It made perfect sense. He was angry about not realizing it much earlier. He felt like a fool! Her bathing suit had fallen off in front of him, and she had made that bizarre comment about the red-light district. He never would have guessed that she actually entered a wet T-shirt contest and slept with other guys down here before she met him! And now, she was mocking his family in front of other people! He wanted revenge, and he wanted it soon! She'd been acting like she was seasick all morning. He wondered if she had actually been on drugs instead. He mistook Elizabeth for a sweet little southern girl and had almost fallen for her. He was angry about offering to take her to dinner, instead of spending his last night with his best friends. He wanted to make it up to them. This was outrageous. Nobody made a fool out of Chad Patterson—nobody!

Chad returned to the beach and buried his head in his hands.

"You've been gone for a while. What happened to Elizabeth?" Eric asked.

"Don't mention her name to me. I'm so mad I can hardly speak!"

"What happened?" Eric moved over next to him.

"She's making a fool out of me! She mocked my sister, and she did it in front of other people."

"No, she didn't! Do you want us to go up there and kick her ass?" Eric shouted.

Chad uncovered his face, sat back slowly, and managed to smile. "That's it! This is simply perfect. I have a plan!"

Luke, Eric, and Steve grinned at each other. Eric rubbed his hands together. "We love it when you have a plan. Tell us please."

Chad told them about the conversation between the guys by the pool. Everything that he was explaining was a misinterpretation of reality. His perception of Elizabeth was severely tainted.

Eric, Luke, and Steve were angry with Elizabeth as well. They wanted revenge.

Chad apologized for taking Elizabeth seriously in the first place, and offered to make it up to them. He wanted to go to the strip club that night. He never mentioned how Elizabeth denied mocking his sister. That lame excuse she had about her untimely smile no longer seemed relevant. Chad believed Sandy and Rebecca instead of Elizabeth. He also wrongly believed that the guys by the pool had been talking about Elizabeth. It never occurred to him that they could have been discussing anyone else.

Chad certainly couldn't believe anything Elizabeth said from that point forward!

Eric commented, "Chad, we've been curious about Elizabeth ever since her comment about the red-light district. We're not surprised by any of this. We're just glad you figured it out. You've been thinking with the wrong head, buddy. It happens. When you get home, you've got Jan waiting for you. We're here to help you celebrate! Now tell us your plan."

"Elizabeth doesn't know that I'm on to her—and she's not going to find out. Do you understand?"

They nodded.

"She still trusts me right now, which is a wonderful thing! When we get back from the strip club tonight, we'll be revved up, right?"

They all nodded.

"I'll make sure she's waiting for us when we get back to the motel. Do you see where I'm going with this? Do I have to spell it out for you?"

They understood.

Chad continued, "And here's a bonus. I called my dad this morning to tell him I'd met a sweet southern girl, which made him very happy. I told him I needed extra cash to take her out to a nice restaurant. He wired me two hundred dollars this morning. So guess what we can do with that extra cash now? The strip club is my treat tonight. Your money is no good! Have I redeemed myself yet for my foolishness?"

"You're fine. You really don't have to do that," Steve answered.

"She'll be waiting for us when we get back from the strip club. I'll make sure of it! We'll get revenge and relief—double pleasure! We'll kill two birds with one stone."

They had been talking all week about the beautiful efficiency of killing two birds with one stone. It was becoming a competition to see who could kill the most birds with one stone.

Fasten your seat belts! It's gonna be a bumpy night!" Chad sneered.

"There you go again with those movie lines!" Steve acknowledged.

Everyone laughed.

"I can't help myself. They just pop out of me. I know every movie line in every movie."

"You know every movie line in every movie that's ever been made?" Luke asked sarcastically.

"Watching movies is my only pastime with my sister. Mary loves it when I act out the characters for her. It's the only way I can get a reaction out of her. You should see her. She smiles and comes alive whenever I do that," Chad admitted.

"How are we going to keep all of this hidden?" Eric asked.

"We'll destroy the evidence," Chad exclaimed. "And Elizabeth already gave us a scapegoat. Remember the fat guy she pissed off at the belly flop contest? He's coming after her."

***

While Elizabeth took a walk along the beach to calm her spirits, Sandy and Rebecca showered and went to happy hour. They were looking forward to seeing Eric, Chad, Steve, and Luke again. Elizabeth returned to the motel room a short time later to take a shower.

Rebecca had been smoking pot earlier that afternoon, and had finally shared some with Sandy. She had been getting it all week from a guy she met after the wet T-shirt contest. The contest had turned out to be the best part of Rebecca's week. She came away with plenty of spending money—and she had been having great sex ever since. But she knew it wouldn't last much longer. After this semester, her college life would be over. She needed to live it up while she still could. She had never quite grasped the college classroom experience. Even with a part-time course load, she couldn't figure out exactly how to study. Actually going to class would have helped, but she could never concentrate whenever she did go to class. She couldn't find the discipline. She had tried, but her social life kept getting in the way.

"Do you think Elizabeth was really mocking Chad's sister?" Sandy asked Rebecca. "She sure did deny it, didn't she?"

"Oh, I forgot about that," Rebecca answered.

They both laughed hysterically. They were still high. "When Elizabeth smiled like that ... oh my God!" They continued laughing and slapping the bar. They ordered another round of drinks.

"I'm having so much fun down here!" Rebecca laughed. "I have a confession, Sandy."

"What is it?"

"I've officially flunked out of school after this semester, and I'm not coming back next year. That's why I'm living it up down here. Stick a fork in me. I'm done. Please don't tell anybody," Rebecca said sadly.

Sandy reluctantly replied, "Actually, I have the same confession, but I'm hiding it quite well. I've been telling everybody that I'm transferring because I want to get back closer to home, but I'm really failing a couple of classes. I'm still trying to pull through. I'll hopefully get my grades up at community college and come back. Perhaps you could do that too? I totally understand how you feel." She pleaded to Rebecca, "Oh, please don't tell Chad and his friends. Good Lord. They're all Ivy League. I told them earlier this week that I'm a straight-A student. They'll probably be coming over here soon."

"Oh, of course I won't. This is our little secret. And we'll be okay. We'll find something else to do with our lives—something better than this," Rebecca exclaimed with a smile.

"Absolutely!"

They made a toast to better days ahead.

Chad, Eric, Luke, and Steve soon entered the bar and walked over to Sandy and Rebecca. They seemed ready for a night out on the town.

"Where are you guys going tonight?" Sandy asked.

"Chad leaves tomorrow. We're taking him to the best strip club we could find around here. This could be the last night we ever spend with him as a single man. He's about to get engaged," Steve answered.

Sandy and Rebecca already knew about Chad's pending engagement. "That's awesome. Blow it out! Have fun!" They laughed. "All good things must come to an end."

"Sandy, I like that shirt better than the one you were wearing the other night," Eric remarked.

"I'm a fashion major. You're not allowed to tease me about my clothes." Sandy laughed.

"A fashion major, really? What are you planning to do with that?" Chad asked.

"I want to be a fashion designer in New York, of course." Sandy was from Long Island.

"That's cool!" Eric replied.

They didn't realize that Sandy was simply covering for herself because she didn't want to be teased any further about the shirt she'd worn several nights before. It was much less likely that they'd tease her about her clothing if they believed she was a fashion major. She had borrowed one of Elizabeth's shirts, a navy blue blouse with soft ruffled sleeves, and a high ruffled neckline. She hadn't admitted it was Elizabeth's shirt because she had already made a previous point that she never borrowed anyone else's clothes. Sandy needed to keep her lies straight, but they were beginning to spiral out of control.

Steve inquired, "Do you know where you want to work?"

"One day at a time right now. My parents are networking for me. I'll have something lined up by the time I graduate." Sandy winked at Rebecca.

"Tell us about Elizabeth. Where did you find that girl?" Eric asked.

"What do you mean?" Sandy and Rebecca looked at each other curiously.

"She was mocking Chad's sister earlier today. That is so wrong!"

Sandy and Rebecca had been high at the time and had misread Elizabeth's smile.

"Well, we were surprised by that too!" Sandy laughed.

They didn't want to admit that they were wrong or high on marijuana.

"We were also wondering, why would she mention a red-light district to us? What's up with that?" Luke asked.

Sandy and Rebecca laughed hysterically again. The question didn't make sense to them. "Red-light district? Are you serious? What did Elizabeth say about a red-light district?"

"Okay, here's the bigger question. Where did you find her? Did you pick her up on the side of the road or something?" Eric shouted.

"Well, of course we picked her up on the side of the road," Sandy answered sarcastically. "Where do you think we found her?" She winked at Rebecca.

Chad overheard and came over.

Sandy continued, "We picked Elizabeth up on the side of the road because she wanted to come down here and turn a few tricks.

That must be why she mentioned the red light district to you. You haven't figured this out already?" Sandy didn't think they'd believe her, but Chad was actually falling for it.

Rebecca kicked Sandy and whispered, "That may not be a good idea. Don't tell a bunch of guys going to a strip club that she's a prostitute."

The guys walked away and started whispering.

Sandy laughed. "These guys are harmless. You should know that by now, Rebecca."

Rebecca wasn't sure. She didn't want to put Elizabeth in harm's way, but she was too drunk and too high to think about it.

Sandy believed it was all very funny.

Chad walked back over to them and asked, "You seriously picked her up on the side of the road? Was she hitchhiking? Why would you all do that? I thought she was one of your friends from school."

"Nope. She's not a girl either. She's twenty-five years old." Sandy shook her head, as if Chad should know better. She was certain he would eventually figure out that she was teasing him. Sandy decided that her fun was just beginning.

Chad stated in a daze, "She seemed like a sweet southern girl at first."

"Oh, she's not even southern, Chad. She's from New Jersey." At this point, Sandy was certain that Chad would figure out she was teasing since Elizabeth had a very distinct southern accent.

"Really? New Jersey? Her accent seems genuine," he said as he walked away.

Sandy was astonished that Chad believed anything she said. "Rebecca, I have a plan for later. Don't let me forget."

"I'll probably forget," Rebecca replied. "I'm getting wasted."

Chapter 6
The Master Plan

Chad walked out of the bar, placed his hands on his knees, and took a deep breath. He needed to remain calm in order to keep his plan in motion. The only way that he could possibly follow through with his plan was to maintain Elizabeth's trust. He walked down the sidewalk and knocked softly on her door.

Elizabeth had just stepped out of the shower when she opened the door. She was wearing shorts and a T-shirt, and her hair was soaking wet. She seemed ecstatic to see Chad.

"May I please come in?" he asked.

"Of course," she replied, opening the door for him to enter.

"Look. I'm sorry about our miscommunication earlier. I'm leaving tomorrow and need to get a good night's rest. Would you like to go out for a quick bite? No five-star restaurant or anything—maybe a slice of pizza or something? There's a pretty good place about a block from here."

"Sure. Anything is fine."

"I'll be back in about twenty minutes. Can you be ready by then?"

"Yes, of course."

As he turned away, she commented on his brown leather shoes. "I like your shoes."

"You don't know when to quit, do you?" He managed a small smile to keep his cover, but he was angry about her comment.

"What's wrong?" Her face straightened.

"Nothing's wrong," he answered. "You like my shoes, huh?"

"I have a serious shoe fetish. Yours are really cool," she answered.

"Thank you," he said. "I'll see you in twenty minutes." He shut the door and walked away. Chad knew the expression from a recent *Saturday Night Live* episode. The show had recently been doing spoofs on the expression, I like your shoes. The hidden meaning was plain and simple. It meant: I want to have sex.

As he walked away and up to the third floor, he felt pleased that the first step toward his revenge plot had been taken. The wheels were in motion. Elizabeth still had no idea that he was going to a strip club that evening. His plan was coming together better than he could have ever imagined.

Chad wondered if Sandy or Rebecca had told Elizabeth about his family's fortune. He surmised that one of them must have surely told her because he had not. He couldn't think of any other reason why a working prostitute would give him so much attention for no financial gain. And why did a prostitute refuse to have sex with him last night? Surely there was a logical explanation. He surmised that she was a true professional. He liked nice girls. She had been playing the part of a sweet, naïve southern girl all along, and she did it well. She clearly had a vivid imagination, and enjoyed role-playing for him. She managed to fool an Ivy League psychology major in the beginning. It made him angry. Nobody made a fool out of Chad Patterson—nobody!

Chad changed into long pants, a long-sleeved shirt, and different shoes. He explained to the others that he needed to spend a little more time with Elizabeth before they left for the strip club. The strip club show didn't begin until ten. They still had plenty of time. Spending the extra little time with Elizabeth was the only way that his plan would ultimately work. He needed her total trust.

***

As Elizabeth shut her door, she felt a renewed sense of relief and excitement. She couldn't wait to spend more time with Chad! He was charming, brilliant, gorgeous, and funny—not like anyone she had ever met. She loved his Boston accent. He was the highlight of her week. And he clearly no longer thought she had mocked his sister. She was relieved. *What a nightmare that had been!* She needed to hurry up and get ready for him! Her heart was racing.

Elizabeth had never been told by anyone that Chad was about to get engaged—or that he planned to have a wild bachelor party tonight as part of his celebration.

Elizabeth didn't understand Chad's odd response to her comment about his nice leather shoes. She didn't watch *Saturday Night Live* regularly and wasn't aware of the hidden meaning behind the expression, I like your shoes.

While Elizabeth was getting ready, Sandy and Rebecca came back from happy hour. They were very drunk. Elizabeth was sober, but she had grown accustomed to this ongoing dynamic with everyone around her.

"Where are you going?" Sandy asked.

"Chad and I are going to get a bite to eat. He's coming back here to pick me up in a few minutes. I'm pretty excited about it."

"Are you sure about that, Elizabeth?" Rebecca asked, seeming surprised.

"Of course I'm sure. He just left here a few minutes ago. He's coming right back."

Sandy whispered, "Rebecca, he thinks she's a prostitute. Let's have fun with this."

"Are you sure you want to keep this up? That might be a bad idea," Rebecca answered quietly.

Sandy ignored her response and turned to Elizabeth. "I want you to look good for Chad tonight. Why don't you let me fix your hair?" Sandy began fluffing Elizabeth's hair and spraying it with hair spray. She grabbed a comb and teased it higher and higher. "Your hair looks awesome, Elizabeth. Let's make it really big. And you need more makeup."

Sandy went into the bathroom and grabbed her own makeup. She told Elizabeth to sit on the edge of the bed as she dabbed blue eye shadow across Elizabeth's eyelids and spread extra blush across her cheekbones. "You have beautiful high cheekbones. We should highlight them!"

Soon thereafter, Lacey and Sue came in from happy hour, and Molly returned from West Palm Beach. They all stared at Sandy and Elizabeth in puzzlement.

"Elizabeth, you're wearing too much makeup," Lacey finally said.

Elizabeth jumped up and looked in the mirror. She grabbed a tissue and started wiping her face.

Sandy looked back toward them and whispered, "Shush! I want to make her look like a prostitute. It's a practical joke that we're playing on Chad. He thinks she's a prostitute."

There was immediate disagreement about what was happening, but Sandy convinced them that everything would be fine.

Elizabeth was wearing a pair of loose white capri pants. She grabbed one of her shirts from a hanger. She decided to wear her navy blue blouse with soft ruffled three-quarter-length sleeves and a high ruffled collar. This was a trendy shirt in South Carolina, but she hadn't seen anyone wearing the style in Florida. She pulled it off of the hanger and started to put it on. Sandy had borrowed it a few days earlier.

"No! You can't wear that shirt!" Sandy shrieked.

"Why?" Elizabeth laughed. "It's my shirt, and I want to wear it tonight. It's one of my favorite shirts."

Sandy pleaded, "If you wear that shirt, tell Chad that it's mine. Please tell him it's my shirt!"

Elizabeth laughed, "You're drunk, aren't you? I won't lie about my shirt."

Sandy suddenly exclaimed, "You can't wear flat shoes! You need to wear high heels." She scurried around the room searching for high heel shoes.

"I didn't bring any high heels," Elizabeth replied. "This is a lazy beach week."

Sandy looked toward Lacey and asked, "Aren't those your high-heel shoes over there? You two wear the same size, don't you? Can Elizabeth please borrow your high heels?"

"I don't want to wear high heels. I like my flip-flops," Elizabeth interjected. "We're just going to a pizza place."

"Don't you want to look good for Chad? I'm helping you out here," Sandy insisted.

Elizabeth was beginning to wonder if Chad was actually planning to surprise her and take her to the five-star restaurant after all. *Maybe he told Sandy.*

Lacey told Elizabeth that she could borrow her high heeled shoes.

"Why do you both want me to wear these shoes?" Elizabeth asked.

"They look great on you," Sandy proclaimed. "You look absolutely great! But you need to tell Chad that you're wearing *my* shirt! It's really important! I have a better idea. Why don't you wear a different shirt?" She hurried toward the closet to find a different shirt.

There was suddenly a knock on the door, and Rebecca answered.

Chad acknowledged Rebecca and said, "I'm here to see Elizabeth."

When Elizabeth came to the door and stepped out to greet him, Chad's eyes widened.

"Do I look bad?" she asked.

"No, actually you look … great," Chad replied with a smile. "You look different with all that makeup."

Rebecca and Sandy watched Chad's reaction through the window. When his eyes widened, they laughed hysterically.

As Elizabeth and Chad walked down the street, he remarked, "You have really high cheekbones. That massive amount of blush you're wearing highlights your cheekbones. I didn't notice them before."

"Is that supposed to be a compliment?" she asked.

"Take it however you'd like," Chad replied.

"Let's not discuss my appearance. Thank you for not giving up on me today. I could tell all along that you're really a nice guy. By the way, what are you majoring in? You spoke about becoming a doctor, but you never told me about your major or what kind of doctor you'd like to become."

"Why don't you tell me about your major instead, Elizabeth? You're in school, right?"

"I've changed my major once already, and I might change it again. Right now, my major is theater."

Chad's eyes widened again.

"Why are you looking at me like that?" Elizabeth asked.

"Why didn't you tell me that last night? You should have told me that last night!"

"We didn't talk about our majors last night. You still haven't told me yours."

"Why did you choose *that* major, Elizabeth? You're role playing for me again, aren't you?" he smiled.

"I started out as a business major, but didn't like it. Then I switched to theater. A couple of adults told me that I should consider pursuing it as a career. And that's what I'm thinking about doing for now, but I'm really not sure what I'll do with it. I don't have my whole life figured out in the same way you do."

Chad laughed. "At this rate, you'll make it all the way to Broadway."

Elizabeth was becoming immune to bizarre replies. Chad had been drinking. She trusted him. She responded, "Tell me about your major at Boston College."

Elizabeth's belief that Chad was a student at Boston College would help him keep his full identity a secret.

Chad smiled confidently. "There's a reason I didn't tell you about my major before, Elizabeth. It's psychology."

"That's awesome. Why didn't you want to tell me that you're a psychology major?"

"Because psychology majors don't usually like to tell people that we're psychology majors. It makes other people uncomfortable."

"I never realized that. Sue is a psychology major, and I've never seen her hide it from anybody. Do you want to become a psychiatrist?"

"No. I want to do research and teach."

They walked inside the pizza restaurant and sat down. Chad said, "I'll have two slices of pepperoni. What are you having?"

"I'll have one slice of cheese pizza."

"And we'll both have water," he said.

Elizabeth tried not to look or feel offended. She wasn't accustomed to being pampered, but that seemed rude. She made excuses for Chad in her mind. Maybe he was simply being frugal in the same way she had been frugal all week. She could have paid for her own meal. But if he really needed to be this frugal, why had he originally asked her to go to the expensive restaurant? Perhaps he changed plans because he couldn't afford the expensive restaurant after all? She had been sober all week. What difference did it really make if she drank water again anyway?

The waiter brought their pizza and waters.

Elizabeth took a small bite and immediately lost her appetite. She pushed it away. She had eaten crackers after being seasick, and the pizza was the first thing she'd tried to eat since then. The sight of a pizza made her nauseous.

"What's wrong? You don't like the pizza?" Chad asked.

"Everything's fine. Thank you for getting it for me, but I've lost my appetite for some reason. You can have it." She took a sip of water. "This water's really good though. Thank you for ordering it for me."

"We don't need to be drinking alcohol right now. I had three drinks at happy hour, and the night is still young. I've got a big appetite right now." Chad grabbed Elizabeth's pizza and devoured it. "I love to eat!" He took another big bite.

"Well, it doesn't show. You're in really great shape," Elizabeth responded.

"Thanks. So what inspired you to major in theater?" he asked curiously.

"When I was younger, I did some community theater and sang in my church choir. I suppose that was my original inspiration."

Chad took a deep breath. "You sang in your church choir? Tell me about that."

Elizabeth was tired of talking about the boring details of her life, but loved that Chad was taking such a personal interest in her. She wasn't accustomed to it. "You really don't want to know about my church youth choir experiences. That's boring stuff."

"Of course I do. What were some of the songs you sang? Did you do anything interesting with your choir?"

"Oh, we spent two summers doing musicals all around the Southeast. Now that you mention it, that experience was really quite awesome." Elizabeth had enjoyed traveling to Alabama, Louisiana, Mississippi, and Georgia.

"What kind of musicals did you do?"

"We did one musical called 'The Boy Who Caught a Fish' and I actually played the lead. I was 'The Boy.'"

Chad stared at Elizabeth's hair, makeup, and breasts. "*You* played a boy?" He sat back, laughed, and shook his head. "How exactly did you pull that off?"

"Oh, it was when I was much younger. I pulled my hair up and wore a burka-looking thing over my head the whole time. We all wore robes. We were in Biblical times. It was easy. I sing alto anyway."

"Oh, I see. What were some of the songs you sang?" Chad asked.

"They were original songs from that particular musical. You probably wouldn't know any of those old songs. This song wasn't in the musical, obviously, but we rode around on those hot buses and sang "The House of the Rising Sun." We must have sung that song a million times. One of our choir directors loved to play it on his guitar, and he'd ask us all to sing along. That was the summer we traveled to New Orleans."

Chad stood up. "That's awful!"

"Why is that awful? What's wrong with you?"

"I know what that song's about. You just went through that whole story so that you could mention that song?"

"No, we sang that song because it was about New Orleans—and that's where we were. That's all. 'Mothers tell your children not to do what I have done,'" Elizabeth explained. The choir director had told them the song was about gambling, and had warned them that gambling was a bad habit.

***

Chad was convinced that Elizabeth was a prostitute who was simply role-playing with him. He loved theater, music and the church, and was convinced that she had a vivid imagination by pretending to be a theater major and church choir singer. He was angry that she was mocking God, but tried his best not to become visibly angry. He knew this particular song, "The House of the Rising Sun," was actually about a house of ill repute. He was certain that Elizabeth was displaying a sick sense of humor by making fun of religion and interjecting her disgusting profession into a discussion about the church.

"Have you spent any time on Bourbon Street?" he finally asked. "Is that what you're saying?"

"Bourbon Street?" Elizabeth asked.

"Isn't that the name of that wild street down there in New Orleans? Yes, it's Bourbon Street. That's where you went!" he demanded.

"Oh no, I don't think so. We toured around the French Quarter. Now that you mention it, we weren't allowed to walk down some of the streets. I remember being curious about them though."

"Oh, I get it now! You're the sweet little southern girl again, the one I like so much, aren't you?"

"If you say so," Elizabeth answered.

Chad looked at his watch. "Let's start walking back toward the motel."

As they strolled down the sidewalk, Elizabeth told Chad that he seemed uptight. She asked if he was stressed about traveling, and rubbed his back to calm him.

Chad was pleased that Elizabeth still trusted him. He had almost lost his temper several times. "Yes, that must be it. I'm stressed about traveling," he responded.

"I'll still have another day and night after you leave. I must admit that I'll miss you when you're gone."

"You think so?"

"It hasn't been perfect, but I've never met anyone else like you. And I absolutely adore your Boston accent."

Chad was certain that Elizabeth was being sarcastic again! He had never known anyone who enjoyed the sound of a Boston accent. He despised his accent. He had never told Elizabeth that he was born in England and spent the first years of his life there before moving to Massachusetts. He had lost his beautiful English accent at an early age. His family had moved to the United States after finding better care for his sister. During his first few years of school in the United States, he had been bullied for having a *sissy* English accent, as well as having a *retarded* older sister. It had been a brutal transition for Chad and his family. He chose not to tell Elizabeth about any of it. He had no tolerance for any person who made fun of his accent or his older sister. From his perspective, Elizabeth had done both.

"You like my Boston accent? I don't think I've heard that one before," Chad replied.

"That's because you're usually around people with your same accent, right?"

"I suppose," Chad remained calm from the outside. She had an answer for everything.

"Are you ready to leave Florida? Do you want to get home?" Elizabeth asked.

"Oh no, not at all. I'm not ready to leave yet. I still have tonight!" he smiled.

Elizabeth smiled back at him.

As they returned to the motel, Chad mentioned, "I need to go study for a while." He looked at his watch. It was eight forty-five. He had plans to be at the strip club by ten. It was only a couple of blocks away.

"Study? What? You need to go study right now?" Elizabeth seemed surprised.

Chad was concerned that he might be losing his cover and laughed. "Yes, I really do need to study. I'll come back to see you after a little while. I promise." He was proud of his cover and didn't consider it a lie because he planned to study the dancing girls at the strip club.

Elizabeth grabbed his hands, squeezed them, and asked, "How can you possibly be planning to study right now? You've had a few drinks. And you'll have all those hours on the plane tomorrow when you can study. This is your last night here. This makes no sense at all."

"I'm actually working on a project, and those guys have been helping me with it. We won't be able to work on the project tomorrow. I promise that I'll be back to see you later—after I study." He smiled at his clever response.

Elizabeth squeezed his hands. "I'm going to miss you terribly after you leave tomorrow."

"Is that your shirt?" Chad asked.

"Yes, this is my shirt. Why?" she asked.

"I was simply asking. I've heard that you all have been wearing each other's clothes."

"Oh, we have, but this is my shirt. Do you really need to study tonight?"

"Yes, as a matter of fact, I do. I really must finish my project."

"What sort of project? Can I help?" she asked.

Chad laughed. "I don't want to get into the details of it right now. Those guys are already helping me. We may have a way for you to help us later though. I promise." He was pleased with his clever cover. He was telling the truth—in a sadistic way.

"You're such a disciplined gentleman. I'm very impressed." She held his hands and looked into his eyes.

Chad gazed into her eyes. He was physically attracted to her. "You're beautiful," he said without thinking about how much he despised her actions.

Elizabeth smiled up at him as they began to kiss. Their physical chemistry was undeniable. They stood in front of the doorway and pulled each other close. Elizabeth caressed his back and shoulders before pulling him closer.

Their kiss grew more passionate. "You feel really good right now," she gasped.

"Don't say that to me. Is that what you say to all those other guys too?"

"What other guys?"

"Are you going to tell me that you haven't been with any other guys this week?"

"Where did you get that crazy idea? I haven't been with any other guys down here! You're the best thing that's happened to me all week. You're the best thing that's happened to me in a very long time. I can promise you that."

***

Elizabeth's heart was racing. Chad's embrace was warm and invigorating. His kiss was tender. It had been a very lonely week for her. Everyone had gone their separate ways for the evening, and she felt safe and secure with Chad. He was smart and strong, and she trusted him in spite of his occasional quirky remarks. He seemed genuinely interested in everything about her.

They kissed again and held each other close. He delicately rubbed his fingers along her back and through her hair, causing her spine to tingle. She wanted to please him. She wanted the pain from the day to fade away into his embrace. For a moment, it felt as though they were the only two people on the planet.

A crowd of people brushed past them on their way to the pool bar. One of them shouted, "Get a room!"

Elizabeth was breathless. "Would you like to come inside for a few minutes? There's no one here. They're evidently all out for the evening."

***

Chad couldn't believe his good fortune. Elizabeth actually wanted him before going to the strip club! He looked at his watch. It was almost nine. His original plan had been to lure Elizabeth up to their room after they returned from the club, but Elizabeth wanted him now! He wondered if Luke or Steve or Eric would want to rape her before the strip club. He wanted to find out.

"Can you walk with me upstairs for a moment? It will only take a second. I promise." He smiled.

"Aren't your friends up there right now?" Elizabeth asked.

"Yes, does that bother you?"

"It doesn't really bother me, but…"

"…Come with me. I have one little thing I need to take care of first."

Elizabeth seemed reluctant at first, but walked up to Chad's room with him. "Step inside for a moment while I grab something from my bag. Don't pay any attention to those guys."

Chad wanted his friends to get a glimpse of Elizabeth in her high-heeled shoes, fluffy hair, colorful makeup, and the ruffled shirt. Chad motioned for them all to remain silent. "Do you like Elizabeth's shirt? That's Elizabeth's shirt," Chad said as he walked toward his suitcase and reached into it. He watched them for a reaction. From their perspective, it proved she was a liar. They all believed that Elizabeth was wearing Sandy's shirt. Chad was using it as yet another weapon to antagonize their hatred toward Elizabeth. He was enjoying himself. The more they hated Elizabeth, the more likely they would follow through with their grand plan to rape her.

Eric, Luke, and Steve were beginning to get visibly angry, but Chad jumped up, turned his back to her and calmed them down, before turning back toward Elizabeth, "Do you mind stepping outside for a moment? I need to ask these guys a quick question."

Elizabeth waved good night to them before stepping out to the breezeway. She shut the door behind her.

Chad asked excitedly, "This is working out better than I ever could have imagined! Did you just see that? Look at her! And she wants me—not later—but now! She's right outside that door. We don't even need to go to the strip club. I can ask her to come right back in here, and we can get started with our plan!"

"I don't think so," Luke said. "We'll be much more fired up to do that after the strip club, don't you think?"

Eric added, "I get it. You're excited, but we've been planning all week to go to the strip club. If she wants you now, she'll want you later too. Anyway, we can buy a few things at the strip club if you know what I mean. I want to make that girl pay for how she's been treating you. She needs to learn a lesson."

Steve remarked, "We're not canceling our plans again tonight because of her. We were all supposed to go to that five-star restaurant last night, and you bailed out on us after you met her. Look how that worked out."

Luke commented, "I'm with Eric. That's the sort of thing you do after a strip club—not before."

"Okay, you're right. It was just a thought. I'll be back in a few minutes," Chad answered. "I have a tendency to do everything bass ackwards anyway." He stepped outside and smiled at Elizabeth, "Let's go back downstairs."

Elizabeth opened her door, and they stepped inside. A couple of people were walking by.

"I should have spent more than five dollars on you tonight," Chad remarked.

Elizabeth laughed before shutting the door. "That sounds

terrible. That sounds like you're spending five dollars on a cheap prostitute."

"What?" Chad looked around and thought Elizabeth was trying to cover for herself in front of the people nearby, by making a joke about prostitution. "Oh, I see. You're being clever, aren't you? Five dollars being spent on a prostitute? That's funny, but I was referring to the pizza slice."

"I realize that you were referring to the pizza slice. What else would you be referring to?"

"My dad would kick my butt if he knew what I was doing right now," Chad remarked.

***

Elizabeth hesitated. Her parents were the last thing on her mind. How could Chad possibly think about his dad at a time like this? But Chad quickly closed the door and wrapped his arms around her. His warm, strong embrace comforted her. His kiss was soft and sweet. In the morning, he would be gone from this place—and she would probably never see him again. She pulled him close as they stood alone in the dark.

"First things first: this shirt has got go! Can we please take it off?" He immediately began to unbutton it. "And I want you to be that sweet little southern girl that you were last night, okay?"

"Well, I am a southern girl, and I'll certainly try to be sweet," she replied.

He smiled down at her. They were soon making passionate love. Elizabeth was overjoyed with their closeness. He felt warm, strong, sensual, and caring.

After a few moments, he asked her do a lap dance for him.

"Lap dance?" Elizabeth didn't like the sound of that at all.

Chad sat up on the side of the bed in the dark room. He reached around, grabbed Elizabeth, and lifted her up into his lap. He was much stronger, but he gently pulled her toward him.

Elizabeth wanted to please him and obliged for a few minutes.

Finally, she said, "I don't like this at all. It just feels dirty and wrong." She gracefully moved away from him while stroking his hair and kissing him gently.

Chad responded, "Ah, I see! You're that sweet little southern girl that I wanted you to be, aren't you? That was brilliant!"

During the next twenty minutes, Chad repeatedly asked her to guide him to the most pleasurable areas of her body, to show him how he could give her the utmost pleasure. He repeatedly asked about her *favorites*. He wanted to fully understand each and every inch of her sensual being.

Elizabeth was overjoyed with Chad's giving nature and genuine care for her pleasure. From her perspective, he was following the same pattern he had been following all along. He wanted to know about all of her favorite things - and this time, they were purely sensual.

***

Chad was preparing to teach Elizabeth a lesson about the pleasure spots she was so readily willing to point out to him. He was preparing to show off his newfound knowledge of Elizabeth's body to his friends. He was preparing to serve her up to them after the strip club. The areas that were now bringing her the utmost pleasure would very soon cause her the utmost pain.

Chapter 7
The Momentum

The room was dark, and time stood still. Elizabeth was ecstatic with joy after giving herself totally to Chad. They had been together in intimacy for a few moments when Chad suddenly sat up and exclaimed, "I need to go work on my project now. I need to leave for a little while, but I promise I'll be back soon."

Elizabeth was disappointed and replied in disbelief, "Can you please work on your project tomorrow? Why don't we take a walk on the beach or go have a drink somewhere?"

"No, I really need to take care of this now. It's important. It won't be the same if I try to do this tomorrow. If you can please be patient and wait here for a little while, I promise I'll be back."

Elizabeth reluctantly agreed, and they got dressed.

Chad opened his wallet and asked, "How much?"

"How much what?" she asked gazing across the dark room toward him.

"You know exactly what I mean. How much do I owe you?"

Elizabeth was stunned for a moment. Why would he owe her money? She remembered their earlier joke about the five dollar prostitute and decided to play along. "Honey, you can run a tab!"

Chad closed his wallet and exclaimed, "Okay, I look forward to seeing you again later this evening."

Elizabeth responded with a gentle touch to his hand and kissed him good night. "Hurry back. I'll be waiting for you here."

Chapter 8
Setting the Stage

Chad was ecstatic as he walked up to the third floor to meet his friends. This was his last night in Fort Lauderdale, and Elizabeth obviously wanted to savor every moment that she could possibly have with him. He had set the stage beautifully for their post-strip club festivities. Elizabeth would be anxiously awaiting their return.

Chad had learned about the act of sexual grooming in one of his psychology classes. He was thrilled that he could apply the technique in his own life. It was the perfect revenge plot. He had learned that sexual predators sometimes employed a grooming technique to lure their targets. They used charm, charisma, and trust. This particular tactic is extremely methodical and manipulative because it often requires the predator to earn the trust of those surrounding the targeted victim, such as friends and family. The best part about the technique was how outsiders often doubted, shamed, and blamed the victims, especially in acquaintance rapes. Outsiders typically viewed acquaintance rapes as less severe. Chad was proud and thrilled that he could channel his specialized knowledge by offering Elizabeth to his friends after the strip club. Her body would be eagerly awaiting all of them. And since she had already had sex with him, she had set the stage beautifully to blame herself when they were done. Chad was certain that they could do whatever they wanted to her.

This plan had started forming long before Chad ever realized it was forming. He was sure that others would blame, shame, and doubt Elizabeth. In the worst-case scenario, he and his friends had powerful parents who would protect them. Their parents trusted them and would never doubt or blame them. He didn't believe that Elizabeth possessed this same luxury. She had insecurities. She had no power. She had given them a scapegoat: the guy from the belly flop contest. The stage was set beautifully, and Chad was thrilled to play the lead role for the remainder of the evening!

Chapter 9
Let's Make a Deal

When Chad returned to his motel room, Eric, Luke, and Steve were anxiously waiting. "I've got her right where I want her! I'm mad, mad, mad—I tell ya!"

"What now?"

"She went through this whole story about how she grew up singing in a Baptist church choir—and played the role of a boy, of all things—only to come back around and tell me they went to New Orleans and sang, 'The House of the Rising Sun!' She made a mockery of the church. How sick is that? I suppose that was her sick way of telling me she's been working as a hooker on Bourbon Street down in New Orleans. She sits around here and spins her little web, thinking the whole world revolves around her. Well, it doesn't. In the whole vast configuration of things, she's nothing but a scurvy little spider!"

"There you go again. I recognize Jimmy Stewart there," Steve exclaimed as they left the motel and walked toward the strip club.

They went out the back gate behind the pool and entered a side street. The bars were all dark inside, and the street was much dirtier than the main strip along the beach. There were bars on most of the windows. A homeless guy was sitting on the sidewalk next to one of the strip club entrances. He asked them for money, but they ignored him and continued walking down the sidewalk.

Even though there were several strip clubs in this area, Eric, Luke, and Steve had selected this particular one earlier in the week. It seemed to be a little cleaner and brighter than the others. It promised to have better-looking girls, and it seemed a little more upscale than the others. It was referred to as a gentleman's club instead of a strip club.

"We picked the best club for you, Chad!" Steve exclaimed.

"Thanks, guys, but remember that I've got this," Chad answered. He paid the full entry fee for all four of them. "Remember our deal? You guys won't allow me to help pay for the motel room. And my dad sent this extra money to me, specifically for tonight. Your money is no good here."

The music was loud in the dim, smoke-filled room. They found a table up front near the stage. Within moments, a tall, thin young woman in tight shorts and a skimpy halter top came over and took their drink orders.

Chad looked around. He wanted this experience to become full preparation for what they planned to do to Elizabeth. This was their foreplay. He was obsessed with his grand plan.

As the waitress returned to the table with their drinks, Chad noticed that the guys were staring at her body. After she walked away, Chad proclaimed, "Just wait until you get back to our motel. Elizabeth's waist is smaller than that. Her body is more muscular than that. I'm really spoiling you guys tonight. And she's back there, waiting for us!" He grabbed his drink, gulped it down, and slammed the empty glass on the table. He caught the eye of their waitress and motioned for her to bring them another round.

The strippers danced around on the stage before venturing around the room.

"Who wants a lap dance?" Steve asked.

"I've already had one," Chad answered.

Luke stared around the room quietly, slowly sipping his drink.

"Are you still on your first drink?" Chad asked. His speech was beginning to slur. "You need a shot!"

Chad ordered a round of shots for the table. The music was growing louder and louder. They could no longer hear each other speak. They observed the girls dancing around the room.

Occasionally one would dance provocatively around the table and swing her hips toward them so they could slip dollar bills into her skimpy lingerie.

"Some of these girls are nasty!" Steve screamed into Chad's ear.

"It doesn't matter. Elizabeth's body is the one waiting for you." He stared blankly ahead as he replied.

After an hour, all the girls gathered on the stage. It was time for the grand finale. Long poles came down from the ceiling, and they danced provocatively around the poles. Disco balls and strobe lights blinked as drunken guys shouted around the room. Suddenly the music stopped, and the whole room went dark. When the lights came back up a few seconds later, the girls were gone. The stage filled with smoke, and an electric guitar roared as everyone left.

"Was that supposed to be some sort of dramatic ending?" Luke asked. "That was lame,"

"Oh, you'll get your dramatic ending, Luke. This whole place is lame compared to what I have in store for us. Don't you worry," Chad replied.

The bouncers demanded that everyone exit toward the back of the building so that a new group of guys could enter through the front entrance for the next show. As everyone approached the exit, they realized they were being led through a souvenir store. It was filled with sex toys, drug paraphernalia, lingerie, and alcohol.

"Of course," Eric replied. "They've got a business to run here, don't they? Check out all this raunchy stuff!"

As they laughed about the various items, Chad had an idea. He approached the young man behind the counter and said, "My girlfriend is really into S&M. What have you got for that? She's really into bondage and appreciates a little pain."

Luke glared at Steve and Eric as Chad purchased a few mysterious gadgets.

The man behind the counter asked Chad if his girlfriend preferred satin ties or rope.

"I'll take both," Chad answered.

"Okay. And over here we have a few sharp metal objects, but they're not too sharp. You do need to be careful."

"Yes, of course. I'm always careful," Chad answered.

"You can take a look at these items and see what you like."

Chad selected a few more items and asked how much he owed.

"Do you want to make a deal? That's a whole lot of stuff," the man asked.

Chad laughed. "Make a deal? What do you mean, like Monty Hall?"

"A lot of people who shop here like to negotiate the total price, especially when they buy that much stuff. That's a lot of stuff you have there."

Chad offered him thirty dollars, and the young man accepted. They walked back toward the motel. It was after midnight.

"Is Jan into S&M?" Luke asked.

Chad laughed uncontrollably. "What? Do you think I was buying that stuff for Jan?"

"You told that guy your girlfriend was into S&M."

Luke was walking behind everyone else.

Chad dropped his bags onto the ground, turned around, and clasped his hands onto Luke's cheeks, staring at him intently. "Luke, wake up! Sometimes I lie to get what I want! I bought this stuff for you! I bought this stuff for all of us, so that we can use it on Elizabeth! And no! Jan is not into this type of stuff. Of course she's not! She's a nice girl!" Chad pulled his hands away from Luke's face.

Luke looked around at everyone else with widened eyes. "Did you all realize this? Are we still really planning to follow through with this?"

"Of course we are!" Steve said excitedly. "She's getting what she deserves. Hey, I have an idea. I need to take a dump. We can put it to good use and smear it all over her when we're finished with her."

"Yes, that will be a symbolic," Eric answered.

"Why wouldn't we follow through with it, Luke?" Chad inquired. "Would you like to know what she said before I left her earlier this evening? She told me to run a tab. You guys are on my tab now—except that she's not getting a dime from any of us! She's getting pain, anguish, and humiliation instead. Do you think she's expecting to make a deal with us?" Chad laughed.

They were stumbling toward the back of the motel. As they walked up the back steps, they saw that Elizabeth's room was dark.

"Are you sure she's waiting for us?" Steve asked.

"Yes, of course. She knows I'm leaving tomorrow. She wants me," Chad said confidently. "Fasten your seat belts. It's going to be a bumpy night!"

"There you go again," Eric laughed. "I recognize that line!"

"I've got one better! I'm Monty Hall now, got it? Are you guys ready to play *Let's Make A Deal?"*

They all replied together, "Sure, let's play!"

"I need your full participation. Here's your line: Hey, Monty! Tell us what you've got behind door number one." Chad pointed toward them to repeat his words.

They all quietly said, "Hey, Monty. Tell us what you've got behind door number one!"

Chad answered, "It's your lucky night, guys! Behind door number one, you have *power*! I want you to reply: Hey Monty! We don't need power! We already have plenty of power! Tell us what you have behind door number two. Okay, repeat that back to me, guys."

"Hey, Monty! We don't need power! We already have plenty of power! Tell us what you have behind door number two!"

Chad replied cheerfully, "Ah! Let's look to see what you have here behind door number two." He pretended to open a door as he looked toward them. "Oh look at that! Behind door number two, you have hate! Do you need any more of that?"

They already knew how to respond, and they were laughing hysterically at Chad's antics. "No, Monty. We don't need what's behind door number two either! We already have plenty of hate!"

Chad happily said. "Okay, so if you don't need any more power and you don't need any more hate, are you telling me that you want what's behind door number three?" He pointed to Elizabeth's motel room door. She was sleeping behind door number three.

"Yes, Monty. We choose door number three! That's all we need! We want what's behind door number three!" They all clapped and laughed.

"Very well then. You already have power and hate. Now you can have what's here behind door number three! Now you'll have everything you need for your perfect rape!" Chad bowed, turned around, and knocked loudly on Elizabeth's door.

Elizabeth was sleeping soundly. Everyone else was still out for the evening. She was a heavy sleeper and didn't hear the knocks at first.

When she didn't come to the door, they all banged on the door and called out her name.

She finally awoke. She had already removed her makeup, and was wearing big, fluffy, comfortable pajamas. Her hair was in disarray. She was hurt that Chad had taken such a long study break after leaving her. She wasn't sure if she should answer the door, especially since she could hear Luke, Eric, and Steve outside too.

They continued knocking, and Steve started walking away. "I need to go take a dump," he said, "I almost forgot." He walked up to their room.

"She can't possibly be in there right now," Eric shouted. "Nobody can sleep through that much noise." They grabbed some nearby pool chairs and brought them by the doorway. "We can wait out here for a little while longer, I suppose. She'll eventually come around."

Chad was annoyed. "She said she'd wait for me here. I can't believe she left."

Elizabeth could hear Chad and his friends, but she couldn't understand what they were saying. She contemplated getting up to answer the door. She wasn't sure if she wanted to see them, especially since she looked awful after sleeping.

Steve returned and told them, "I just took a huge dump. It's stored in a plastic bag upstairs."

They each gave him a high five and laughed hysterically.

Chad sat down and said, "I'm sorry about this, guys. I felt sure she'd be here waiting for us. She'll show up soon. And she trusts me now. I'll ask her to come upstairs where we can easily trap her. After she willingly steps foot onto our turf, especially after she's already had sex with me tonight, nobody will blame us for what we're planning to do. They'll blame her. That's how outsiders view this sort of thing. She has no credibility anyway. We have the power to make this happen with no consequences."

"And don't forget hate! We have hate! Everything we need for the perfect rape!" Luke interjected.

Chad answered, "That's right. Luke, you've got first dibs. Take turns ... as many times as you'd like. I've got rope to tie her down—and satin ties to choke her throat if she tries to bite anybody. If she screams too loud, I have something to calm her down and shut her up. When I went to the bathroom at the strip club, some guy sold me a drug to silence her if necessary. I didn't want to say anything about it while we were in there. I didn't want to scare you."

"You've thought of everything, Chad," Steve said.

"When you're all done, leave me alone with her. I'll do the worst part."

"What do you mean?" Eric asked.

"You don't need specifics. You do your part, and I'll do mine. I simply want to make sure she never has children—that is, if she survives the night and ever wants to have children."

Sandy and Sue came toward them from the front of the motel. "Hey, guys! What are you doing out here?"

"We're looking for Elizabeth. Have you seen her?" Chad asked.

Eric stared at him angrily.

"The last time I saw her, she left here with you. What was that about?" Sandy asked.

Chad answered, "I just wanted to talk with her. That's all. And we'd like to talk to her again right now. Do you know where she went?"

"I really don't know." Sandy placed her key in the door and turned the knob. She didn't know that Elizabeth was inside.

As Sandy entered the room, Chad cried out, "Sandy, we're really worried about Elizabeth! I dropped her off here a few hours ago, and I haven't seen her since!"

Elizabeth overheard Chad's worrisome cry as Sandy opened the door. Elizabeth wanted to console him, to let him know that she was okay, but she didn't want him to see her at the moment.

Chad, Luke, Steve, and Eric decided they could wait a few more minutes. "That was a clever remark," Eric said. "You really sounded like you were worried about her."

"Yes, it was. She could end up missing tomorrow, you know. And we're simply worried about her. That's all. And if she happens to disappear, the world will be a better place," Chad answered.

"Is that what you think? Do you realize that you're thinking like a Nazi now?" Eric asked.

"No, I'm not!" Chad exclaimed.

As Sandy turned on the light in the room, Elizabeth curled into a fetal position, covered herself with a blanket, and slid her head under the pillow. She didn't want to be seen. Elizabeth made an effort to blend in with the rest of the messy room and bed. Sandy walked straight into the restroom, grabbed her lipstick, turned out the lights, and walked outside. "She's not in there."

"Okay, we'll wait a little longer," they guys agreed.

As Sandy walked away, Chad assured his friends, "We only need to do one thing when we find her ... and we will find her! We simply need to lure her upstairs. She trusts me. She's already been inside our motel room twice today. If she willingly walks upstairs and enters our motel room, this rape becomes her fault—not ours! That's how the outside world will view it. And if she disappears after that, we don't know anything about it. Deny. Deny. Deny. She already gave us a great scapegoat—the guy who threatened her after the belly flop contest!"

Chapter 10
The Dark Side Revealed

Elizabeth answered the door to Chad the following morning. She was hurt that he had waited so long to return.

Chad stepped inside and proudly, but softly, proclaimed, "We were going to hurt you last night."

Elizabeth was taken aback. "You did hurt me last night—when you left for all those hours, especially after I had sex with you."

"I'm telling you that we were going to hurt you physically—all four of us."

Elizabeth stepped back. "What do you mean, hurt me? Were you planning to beat me up or something? Why would you do that?"

"No, we weren't planning to beat you up, Elizabeth."

She felt instinctively relieved. "I didn't think you were capable of that."

"Oh, I'm indeed capable of that, and we would certainly beat you up if it weren't so obvious. You'd be walking around here all black and blue today. We're smarter and more subtle than that."

"What a horrid thing to say!"

"Yes. We were going to hurt you physically, and I am telling you that you would have ended up in the hospital last night if my friends and I had gotten our hands on you."

"Dear God! You're insane! Why would you want to do something so horrible?"

"Because of who you are," he quietly responded.

"Can you please be a little more specific? What did I ever do to you? I trusted you. I admired you."

"You deserve it, Elizabeth. The world will be a better place if you're not in it. We're all here to make the world a better place after all, aren't we?"

"You were nice to me last night. I slept with you. You were kind and giving. I thought you cared about me. What changed today?" Her heart was pounding. Her chest was tightening.

"I was setting you up by being nice to you. Don't you understand how that works? I'll be more specific. Before your hospital visit, we were planning to have a little fun first—with a gang bang."

"You were planning to shoot me?" Her eyes widened, and she looked frantically around the room for something to defend herself. She felt short of breath.

Chad gave her an odd look and scratched his head. "Shoot you? I didn't say that. No, we weren't going to shoot you either, Elizabeth. You certainly know what a gang bang is, don't you?"

"No, I don't know what a gang bang is. You weren't planning to beat me up or shoot me? How exactly were you planning to hurt me physically—so badly that I could wake up in the hospital?"

"Wake up? I didn't say that you'd wake up there, did I? Okay, let me explain it to you another way. You were going to have a few layovers before you reached your final destination." He laughed sadistically.

Elizabeth desperately wanted to understand. "You're insane!" She wanted to escape, but he was blocking the doorway. It was daylight, and one of her roommates could return at any time, which gave her a small sense of security. Terrified yet curious, she gathered her composure and asked, "Why would you want to do something horrible to me? Why are you saying this? Are you sober? Are you on drugs?"

"I'm not drunk, and I do not do drugs!" he shouted. "I know exactly what I'm saying!"

As he stood in front of her, her vision blurred. Her body grew weak with fear. She attempted to find a sense of normalcy through his insanity.

"Elizabeth, do you know what rape is?" he asked.

Her stomach felt sick. She had had consensual sex with Chad the night before because she adored him. She thought she'd never see him again after the trip. She considered him to be her only ray of sunshine during a very dark week. "Yes, I know what rape is. I mistook you for a good person, Chad. I thought you cared about me, but last night wasn't rape."

Chad laughed again. "I realize that. I was setting you up, and you almost fell for it. Where did you go last night after I left?"

"I didn't go anywhere. I was sleeping."

"Nobody sleeps through that. We knocked on your door really loud, Elizabeth!"

"I did wake up. I heard you all out there, but I decided not to answer the door. I was hurt that you'd been studying for such a long time. And I really didn't want to see your friends at that point either. They haven't been very nice to me. All of you were banging on the door. That's when I woke up."

"Damn. That's where I went wrong! If I had knocked on the door alone, you would have answered?"

"I don't know. I may have answered the door, but maybe not. Thank God I didn't! I was hurt that you'd been gone for such a long time. I thought you were a normal person—a kind, charming gentleman. When did you turn on me, and *why* did you turn on me?"

"Turn on you? Is that what you think? I was setting you up the whole night. I did that for my friends, Elizabeth. That's what friends do. We look out for each other. Luke was supposed to have you first. He's a virgin, you know. And I'm a giver. My plan was to give you to Luke. You see, I'm generous like that."

"You're evil like that."

"I'm not evil. You are! Let me explain this to you in a different way. Stay with me on this. We're playing *Let's Make A Deal* with Monty Hall now, got it? Behind door number one, we have power." He pretended to shout out into the distance, "Hey Monty! We don't need power! We already have that! What have you got behind door number two, Monty? You've got hate? No! We don't need hate either! We already have that! We want what's behind door number three, Monty!" He stopped and glared at Elizabeth. "You were behind door number three—everything we needed for our perfect rape. Do you understand yet, Elizabeth? We have power and hate. You're the only thing we needed for our perfect rape."

Elizabeth stared at him in disbelief. "You really are insane. Oh my God. I never would have imagined that you could be capable of this."

"Oh, you have no idea what I'm capable of doing. You're supposed to be missing today. The sight of you makes me sick. You shouldn't be walking around here—alive." His demeanor was cold, calculated, and calm. "We should have gang-banged you when we had the chance – when you came up to our room the first time. Do you remember that?"

Elizabeth couldn't understand what happened to the fun-loving adorable young man she had met a couple of days before. She was standing in front of a monster instead of the sensitive, caring person who had seemed interested in the smallest details of her likes and dislikes.

"You're like Dr. Jekyll and Mr. Hyde!" she screamed.

"No, I'm not. Everyone knows that he took a potion. You simply make me angry."

"Well, you're like Ted Bundy, aren't you?"

"No, I'm nothing like Ted Bundy either, Elizabeth. His victims were random. There's nothing random about choosing you."

"Why did you choose me?" She reached for the bedside table. "Why?" Her eyelids fluttered, and her knees weakened. She fell slowly to the floor. Her elbows stopped the fall, automatically propping onto the edge of the bed. Elizabeth was kneeling and clasping her hands, which prompted her to pray for guidance through this horror.

Chad stood above her and said, "I want to make the world a better place, and the world will be a much better place when you're not in it! We were *really* going to enjoy hurting you last night!" He broke into laughter as she grew weaker. He was proud of his power. "And we were going to make sure you never have children. We bought gadgets to help us make that happen. Someone like you should never be allowed to have children … if you had survived, that is. You showed me all your favorite sensual spots, didn't you? I had plans to make those your most painful spots. And you thought I really cared? You see, I'm a good actor too, Elizabeth."

Elizabeth was wearing a bikini and an oversized, long-sleeved linen shirt, which was open in the front. She looked down and noticed her cleavage before pulling the shirt together to cover her body. She felt extremely vulnerable, both physically and mentally. "But you were kind to me last night and the day before. What changed?"

"I was setting you up. You're stupid, Elizabeth. That's why you don't understand. Have you ever heard of sexual grooming? I learned about it in a psychology class. I was grooming you to trust me."

Elizabeth answered, "You do realize that you weren't actually being taught to do that, don't you? You were being taught about that behavior as it pertains to other people … evil people, right? That type of behavior wasn't being condoned in your classroom. Don't you understand the difference between right and wrong?" Elizabeth already knew the answer. She remained on the floor as he gazed down at her with a steely smirk.

"You know, everyone around here is like my puppet on a string. I was looking forward to watching those guys have their way with you last night." Chad moved his hands up and down with his fingers stretched apart. "You were my first puppet when you educated me in great detail about the details of your body. I used that newfound knowledge to motivate my friends. Luke would have been my next marionette. Now where's your sense of humor, Elizabeth? You know how this works, don't you? You say that you're a theater major, right? Don't you know how marionettes work?"

"You really are insane. Why do you hate me so much? What did I ever do to you?"

"I hate you because of who you are!"

"Do you hate theater majors or something?"

"Don't be ridiculous. I don't believe that you're really a theater major. You and I are at war. You're the enemy, and I have powerful allies!"

"So you're like a Nazi?"

"Nazi? That's what Eric said. No, I'm not a Nazi, but you're getting warm. Nazis typically hate people who don't have a choice about who they are. You've made the wrong choices in life. That's why I hate you."

"What sort of choices?"

"Come on. Surely you know the answer to that. I hate you because you leave dirty dishes in the sink! And I hate dirty dishes!"

"That's no reason to kill a person!"

"Stop! This is not about dirty dishes! I just had to throw that in there," he said with a laugh.

Elizabeth tried to stand up, but she was too weak. Her vision blurred again, causing her to fall down onto the bed. She couldn't speak. Her faced turned pale. Her whole body felt cold and limp, and she suddenly passed out.

"What's the matter now? Surely you hear this sort of talk in your world, don't you?" He looked down and shook her, but she didn't wake up. "Thank you, God. Now, if I can find a way to get her up to our room."

The door opened, and Sue walked into the room. "What's the matter with her? Has she been drinking this morning?"

"Yep, that's it. She drank a Bloody Mary on an empty stomach. She'll be all right. I'm looking after her. Don't worry," Chad answered.

"Are you sure she's all right?"

"Yep, I'm taking care of her."

Sue grabbed a bottle of sunscreen. "I forgot this."

"Well, you certainly need your sunscreen in this powerful Florida sunshine!"

When Sue didn't shut the door completely, Chad shut it behind her.

Elizabeth started to awaken.

"Darn, you're waking up?"

"What happened to make you such a monster?" Elizabeth asked weakly.

"The red-light district, Elizabeth," he answered slowly and methodically.

"So now you want to stop this conversation?"

"I didn't say anything about stopping this conversation. I'm having fun," he replied.

"You just mentioned the red light."

"I'm talking about where you live and work—in the red-light district."

"I live in a dorm on campus. What are you talking about?"

"No, you don't. Those girls picked you up on the way down here. What were you doing, hitchhiking?"

"Good God! Where did you ever get that idea? You must have misunderstood something."

"I don't misunderstand anything. I'm a very intelligent guy. Those other girls are not your friends. You live in a red-light district."

"I live with them in a dorm. You and I talked about that when I first met you. You know this already."

"I realize you told me that, but I don't believe anything you say."

"Why would I lie to you about that? If you don't believe me, go ask them."

"Sandy already told me they picked you up on the way down here."

"What? That's impossible. Go ask Danielle or Sue or Molly. I live with all of them in the dorm. Why is this so important?"

"I'll go ask them in a minute. What exactly do you think a red-light district is?"

"It's a stoplight in a traffic intersection. It's also an expression that means that we should stop the conversation."

"Are you serious? You really don't know what a red-light district is?" He scratched his head. "And I've never heard that expression."

"Maybe it's a southern expression."

"How long have you known those other girls?"

"I've known most of them since last year ... almost two years."

"Were you wearing your own shirt last night—or was it Sandy's shirt?"

"It was my shirt. I told you that already."

"Sandy said it was her shirt."

"What does that have to do with any of this horror? I haven't had that shirt for very long. I may still have the receipt in my pocketbook. I bought it on campus."

"Are you trying to be that sweet southern girl again? How old are you?"

"You know how old I am. We already talked about that too. I'm nineteen."

"Last night, I thought you were a twenty-five-year-old hooker from New Jersey."

"Good God. What is wrong with you? I have never been anywhere near a hooker!"

"Yes, you have. They're swarming everywhere around here." He waved his arms in the air.

"I haven't seen any. Maybe there aren't as many as you think either. You thought I was one." Elizabeth's stood up, and they stared at each other in stunned silence.

"If the two of us were a chemistry experiment, this entire motel would have blown to bits just now. You know, this all started yesterday in my room. You said that conversation belonged in the red-light district. Do you remember saying that to me?" Chad asked matter-of-factly.

"Yes. But that was because I wanted you to stop that conversation. I didn't like the direction it was going."

"Listen to me. You need to understand that a red-light district is a section of town where hookers roam, and there are stores that sell porn and sex toys and that sort of thing. It's not something you should bring up in casual conversation."

"I don't go anywhere near places like that. I'm afraid of those places."

"Wait a minute! What about all of that talk about singing 'The House of the Rising Sun'? Was that true?"

"We really sang that song when we were traveling around on the buses in New Orleans. I told you that. What does that have to do with anything?"

"That song is about a house of ill repute!"

"I thought it was about gambling. Our choir director told us that it was about gambling."

"I thought you were telling me that you work as a hooker in New Orleans. I thought you were role-playing with me." He stopped, stared at Elizabeth. "Were you in a wet T-shirt contest down here?"

"No! I was a judge in a belly flop contest. I could never ever enter a wet T-shirt contest."

"Somebody around here was in a wet T-shirt contest, weren't they? It must have been somebody else. Those guys by the pool must have been talking about somebody else. They never said your name. Oh goodness."

Elizabeth didn't tell him that Rebecca had been in the wet T-shirt contest.

"You have got to be the unluckiest person I've ever met! This is a lot of coincidences. Actually, maybe you're the luckiest person I've ever met. Were you really in here sleeping last night?"

"I already told you that."

"You have a guardian angel. Do you know that?"

"I don't feel very lucky right now, Chad. I feel humiliated."

"You look really different today. You look a whole lot better without all that makeup."

"What? Thank you ... I think. I don't normally wear that much. I actually took some of it off before I saw you last night. Sandy kept adding it everywhere. She was trying to make me look good for you."

"What did you say?" Chad's eyes widened.

"Sandy knew that I was about to go out with you, so she fixed my hair and makeup. I think she wanted me to look nice for you."

Chad shook his head and rubbed his forehead. "I was Sandy's puppet. Actually, we both were! Wow. She told me you were a hooker. Then she tried to make you look like one? I can't believe she did that, especially since she knew I was going to a strip club last night."

"You went to a strip club last night?"

"Yes, I did. Everybody knew that except for you." He turned toward the door. "We bought a whole bunch of gadgets to use on you. We need to get rid of that stuff. I need to get to the bottom of this." He stormed out, slamming the door behind him.

Elizabeth took a deep breath. She was humiliated, hurt, and mentally exhausted. She immediately began to blame herself. She didn't know who she could tell about this, if anyone. It was too unbelievable. If she hadn't heard Chad say all of those horrible things, she might have a hard time believing it herself.

***

Chad walked out to the beach and found Sandy. "I have a few questions for you."

"What is it, Chad? Are you looking for Elizabeth again?"

He smirked at her. "I found her. Whose shirt was she wearing last night? And I want the truth."

"Why do you want to know that? Whose shirt did she tell you it was? Chad, I told you earlier that it was my shirt, didn't I?"

"Yes, you did. But is that the truth?"

"I've already told you whose shirt that was," she said.

"Elizabeth says it's her shirt. She told me where she bought it, and she has the receipt for it."

"That bitch!"

"Is that bitch a prostitute as well? You told me that too."

"Chad, I was being sarcastic! I didn't think you'd believe me," Sandy shook her head. "That's ridiculous!"

"Is it really ridiculous? Are you certain about that? I believed you. I had sex with her last night. I thought she was turning a trick."

Sandy stared in disbelief before bursting into hysterical laughter. Tears rolled down her face. "You know, I thought I was playing a little practical joke on you. Oh my God! How did it ever go that far?"

"Oh, you have no idea how far it went. That's just the beginning. What's wrong with you girls? You can't go around joking about that sort of thing! Don't you know that?"

Chad stormed away to his room and told Eric, Luke and Steve that he didn't think Elizabeth was a prostitute after all. "I told her everything! And she's not a prostitute!"

"What do you mean, you told her everything?"

Chad gave them a general overview of his conversation with Elizabeth. "She knows too much now," he exclaimed in a panic.

"Well, naturally, she doesn't want you to think she's a prostitute. She's protecting herself. Think about it," Eric concluded.

Luke, Eric, and Steve explained that she was a very convincing liar. "She obviously doesn't want the world to know she's a prostitute. She's playing you again, and you're falling for it again. There is no way that you could be that wrong about her. You're too smart for that."

***

Elizabeth decided to step outside into the sunshine. She had a newfound appreciation for walking freely outdoors in the open air, but still felt very much alone in a crowded place. She noticed Rebecca and Sue standing on the sidewalk and walked toward them. The world seemed to be moving in slow motion.

"Did Chad take care of you in the room?" Sue asked.

Elizabeth was at a loss for words. *What exactly did Sue mean? Is Sue in on it too?* Elizabeth started to tear up, but she realized that she couldn't talk about it right then. Her emotions were too raw. It felt surreal and beyond comprehension. She couldn't form the words to explain what had occurred in the motel room.

The outside world was filled with warm sunshine and smiling faces. Elizabeth didn't feel as though she belonged there anymore. Her dignity was gone. Everyone she knew lived in a safer superior world, the same world that she had once been a part of—up until that moment. She was in a deep tunnel where others dared not go. She had no idea how to invite anyone else into that cold, dark, disgusting place in order to help them understand. She didn't want to invite anyone else. Chad and his friends weren't planning to rape anyone else except for her. She was isolated. They were kind and gentle to everyone else. How could she possibly explain any of this? She didn't understand it herself.

Elizabeth had already felt very alone, and Chad preyed upon that. He had totally isolated her from the rest of the world. She didn't know how to begin crawling back into the light toward dignity and safety. Elizabeth had always considered herself a strong person with a sense of pride, but this horror was rocking her to the core. She knew Chad and his friends had impeccable reputations and larger-than-life personalities. They were viewed as brilliant, kind, distinguished gentlemen, but Elizabeth knew otherwise. She wasn't sure that anyone would believe her if she tried to tell them otherwise.

Sue finally said, "Hello, Elizabeth? Did you hear me? What was going on in that motel room just now?"

"We were just talking," Elizabeth replied as she looked away. Her face was pale. Being a gang rape target, and being mistaken for a prostitute, filled her with shame and self-blame. She turned around and walked back toward the motel room, trying to appear as normal as possible, but it was far too difficult. She felt branded. She didn't want to be in public.

Sue and Rebecca followed her back to the motel room and found her in bed. "Have you been drinking this morning, Elizabeth?" Rebecca asked.

"No."

"Chad said you had a Bloody Mary," Sue commented.

Elizabeth didn't answer.

"Is there something you're not telling us?" Rebecca asked.

"You wouldn't believe me if I told you."

"Try us."

"Those guys planned to do something really bad to me last night. That's the only way I can possibly describe it right now."

"Why would they want to do something bad to you last night?"

Elizabeth had no idea how to answer the question. Any response placed her on the defensive. It required her to explain her own actions as opposed to their actions. It was a humiliating question. "I really don't know where to begin. I don't understand it fully myself."

"Did you do something to them? Did you make them mad?" Rebecca asked.

"No, I didn't do anything to them." This whole ordeal was growing more difficult. Elizabeth was now being asked to justify their actions. She couldn't. It was a hurdle she didn't expect to jump. What they planned to do was wrong. There should be no excuses for them, but she seemed to be the only person who fully understood it. She had slept with Chad the night before and because of that, she didn't think that anyone would ever take her seriously.

Rebecca responded, "I remember something now. I met a guy, and we were making out in the bushes after midnight. I was wasted but I heard Luke, Eric, Steve, and Chad in the parking lot. They were acting out a scene that sounded like the Monty Hall game *Let's Make A Deal*. They were quiet, and I couldn't understand their words exactly. They were clowning around and having fun. They may have said they were going to do something to you, but they didn't, right? They could never hurt anybody. They're nice guys."

Elizabeth knew otherwise, but what could she do? She remained silent.

Rebecca and Sue went back to the beach.

Chad knocked on the door a few moments later. "Can I talk to you? I won't hurt you."

Elizabeth reluctantly opened the door and stepped outside onto the sidewalk to speak to Chad. Perhaps Rebecca was right.

Chad started, "Look, I had a talk with my friends. They still believe you're a hooker. They still think you're lying. And now I'm not sure either. I don't know what to believe anymore."

"Still lying? What is that supposed to mean? Why am I the bad guy here? And they don't know me. I thought you did."

"It doesn't matter. I'm leaving in a couple hours. Do you know any of their full names? I know that you know mine."

"No, I don't know their full names. How did any of you seriously believe you could have gotten away with doing those horrible things to me? Were you being serious?"

"You still don't get it, do you?"

"No."

"It's about power. We can do whatever we want to you because we have power, and you don't. No court system would ever prosecute us if you tried to press charges, especially for that crime. We can crush your credibility and easily label you a liar. A lawyer would tear you apart, and we'd still walk. This is 1983. It's never worth it for a woman to press charges for rape, especially against a powerful man—or men. There are four of us and one of you. It would be our words against yours. Do you not understand that? Nobody would ever believe you."

"No, I really don't understand. I understand the part about people not believing it. I can hardly believe it myself." Elizabeth's chest was tightening again, and she felt short of breath.

"I had drugs to force on you. You would have had drugs in your system. You could have been portrayed as a drug addict."

"No, that's not true. I've never been a drug addict!"

Chad stopped and said softly, "Those guys by the pool were really talking about somebody else, weren't they?"

"What guys?" Elizabeth asked.

"It doesn't matter. You would have come to our room willingly after having consensual sex with me. You would have had drugs in your system. I'm sorry to tell you this, but everyone would blame you—not us."

Elizabeth thought for a moment. Sue and Rebecca had already asked about her actions, not Chad's actions. They had asked if Elizabeth had done anything to make the guys mad at her. She knew Chad was right.

"You're naïve, Elizabeth. This is how the world works. I didn't make these rules. I simply live in a world where the rules exist. Have you ever heard of Chappaquiddick?"

"Yes…Ted Kennedy wasn't charged with a crime."

"Exactly, do you understand yet?" He paused for moment. "I need to tell you a few more things about me because you'll find out anyway. They're not bad things, but it will help this situation if you know these details now. I'm about to get engaged. And I don't go to Boston College. I'm an Ivy Leaguer. At first, I didn't want to intimidate you with my Ivy League status. And later, it was a nice way to keep my identity concealed…but I suppose none of it matters any more. And I'm about to transfer to a school in England. I was born there, and I look forward to having an English accent again. I hate this Boston accent."

"Well, I really liked your Boston accent," Elizabeth replied. She realized that Chad had been misleading her about many of the details in his life—all while simultaneously accusing her of doing exactly that. He was a hypocrite. She had become their gang rape target, yet she was being portrayed as the wrongdoer. She was surrounded by hypocrites. And those same hypocrites were all banding together against her. Their ability to manipulate was far beyond anything she could comprehend. She didn't know how to battle any of it. It was over her head. They seemed to know much more about the world than she did. And they certainly knew how to manipulate much better than she did.

Chad seemed proud of his brilliance. "If you had survived last night and tried to press charges against me, you would have told them that a student at Boston College did that to you. And by the time anyone would have figured out who I was, or came looking for me - if ever - I would have had to be extradited from England. The American court system would never extradite me, especially with Eric's father on my side. All four of us could easily testify that you came to our room, willingly, after having consensual sex with me, which would easily discredit any accusation you tried to make against us. No court system would ever press charges against us under those circumstances. And if you hadn't survived, there would be no evidence because you would be missing today. I had a plan for everything. You could have easily been labeled a runaway. The guy from the belly flop contest would have been questioned long before any of us would have been suspected of wrongdoing. He's the one who threatened you publicly, right? We've been good to you publicly. Everyone else around here trusts us. We made sure of it. We had all of our bases covered, Elizabeth. You don't understand who you're dealing with here. And I'll be long gone in an hour."

"You're the epitome of evil. Those guys still have another night here—all three of them, don't they? I'll have to stay in this motel with them for one more night."

"That's not my problem any longer. It's your problem now. Actually, it may be their problem too. You know too much about their capabilities now, don't you?"

Elizabeth stared away before replying, "I wish we could go back to this time yesterday. I thought you were an amazing ray of sunshine. I trusted you and adored you. Please tell me that you're not capable of doing this to anyone else, that you almost made one horrible mistake in your life, but didn't." Elizabeth felt extremely isolated. She felt like she was the only person on earth who Chad was capable of hurting. And her subconscious was beginning to feel as though she deserved his abuse.

"I've never done this to anyone else." He stopped suddenly and walked toward her. "Wait a minute. You may be on to something there…never mind, that was a crazy thought."

"What's a crazy thought? What could be any crazier than what has already happened today?"

"I told you too much this morning, and my friends are really mad at me about that. They really could come after you, you know? You know too much. What if I had a way to help you relax and make you forget everything I said this morning? What if I could convince your subconscious that I never said any of those things to you at all?"

Elizabeth immediately liked the sound of this idea. She considered how tainted the world appeared and felt through the eyes of a rape target. If she could erase the horror, it would feel magical.

"Why would you want to do that for me? How exactly could you do that?"

"I wouldn't be doing it for you, although I am beginning to feel a bit sorry for you. I'd be doing it for my friends because you know too much about them right now. I learned how to do something in one of my psychology classes that might work, but you have to be susceptible to it—willing and cooperative. You're good at memorizing, aren't you?"

"I suppose I'm pretty good at memorizing. Yes."

"Look, don't tell anybody about this—nobody! My friends don't believe in this stuff anyway. A lot of people don't. I'm not 100 percent sold on it myself."

"All I really want is for the horror of this trip to go away forever," Elizabeth sighed.

"Well, that's going to be a problem. I don't know how to make this go away forever. You and I will need to agree on a very specific time for the memories to return."

"Okay, let's agree on two hundred years from now. We'll all be gone by then."

"That would take a very long time, and I'm not sure how to do that anyway. I need an ending time to make this work."

"Okay, what about having these memories return when I'm a hundred years old?"

"Don't you have a great grandmother who was born in 1890, and she's still alive?" Chad asked.

Elizabeth had told Chad about her great grandmother when they first met. She was touched that Chad remembered. She wanted desperately to forgive him for what he had almost done to her.

Chad continued, "You may still be alive at age one hundred. Evidently the women in your family live for a long time, don't they? I refuse do this to a hundred-year-old lady."

Elizabeth felt a twinge of normalcy. He viewed her as a human being for the first time today. She responded, "Okay, what about half that amount of time? What about age fifty?" She was looking forward to relaxing, as he was promising, and for the horror of the day to disappear for a long time. At nineteen, age fifty seemed like an eternity from now.

Chad answered, "Well, menopause usually sets in at age fifty. It's not an exact science, but I don't want you to come looking for me with a gun when you're starting menopause. You're going to be really mad at me when these memories come back! You do understand that, right? And when they do come back, it will feel like this is happening to you all over again. I don't want to mix that experience with menopause. Are you absolutely sure you want to do this?"

"Yes, I'm very sure. I want to relax and forget this horror. Okay, what about age forty-eight? That should be two years before menopause kicks in, right? That will give me a couple of years to recuperate before menopause, right?"

Chad smirked. "You have a lot to look forward to, don't you? Like I said, menopause typically begins around age fifty, but it's not an exact science. We can only speculate when it will start. But that's fine. Let's go with age forty-eight. That will be 2012—twenty-nine years from now. Which month do you want? We need to agree on a month in 2012 for the memories to return."

"Let's go with this same month. We can plan for these memories to return in March 2012."

"Okay, I'm getting ready to take care of this. I'll need a few minutes. If anyone asks what I'm doing, tell them I have a headache that I'm trying to get rid of before I travel. Don't interrupt me, got it?"

"Yes, I've got it."

"And I want you to simply think about March 2012—twenty-nine years from now. That's all you really need to do. Just think about March 2012. I'll do everything else. Got it?"

"Yes, I've got it."

Chad sat down on the sidewalk, pulled his knees toward him, and propped his elbows upon them. He rubbed his temples intensely. His eyes were closed; he appeared to be concentrating deeply. Elizabeth paced the sidewalk and became lost in the thought of forgetting about this traumatic day—at least for the next twenty-nine years.

Within fifteen minutes, Chad stopped rubbing his temples, opened his eyes, and attempted to stand. His eyes were glassy. He was dizzy and stumbled around before leaning against the wall.

Elizabeth asked, "Are you okay? That was amazing. Do you think it worked?"

Chad stared at her in a daze. When he finally managed to speak, he asked, "How long was I doing that? Did you think about March 2012?"

"Yes, I repeated it at least a hundred times. I've been pacing back and forth thinking about nothing else for the past fifteen minutes." Elizabeth felt elated.

"You only needed to think about it once or twice, but okay. That could really work. Anyway, I planted a few extra surprises in there for you," he laughed sadistically.

"What is that supposed to mean?"

"I needed an insurance policy in case you ever decide to talk. I can't believe you let me do this to you. Why do you still trust me?"

"I thought this was supposed to help us—all of us."

"It will. Don't worry. I can't cause you to hurt yourself, but I might be able to make you release your inhibitions if you ever decide to talk about this."

"Well, if I don't remember anything that you said to me this morning in that motel room, how could I possibly ever talk about it? Nobody else knows about it except for you, me, and your friends, right? I feel certain that you and your friends won't tell anyone either."

"I suppose you're right." He looked into Elizabeth's eyes and said, "But just in case, if the subject of our rape plot arises within the next twenty-nine years, you will respond, 'Maybe I would have enjoyed it.' And you will act like a prostitute."

Elizabeth gasped, "That's impossible! I'll never do either of those things...but it doesn't matter. The subject could never possibly come up."

"You'll remember me as nothing more than a kindhearted, distinguished gentleman—your thoughts of me before I told you about our plans. And you won't remember my friends at all if this stuff works."

As Elizabeth walked away from him, she thought again about March 2012. It would be another lifetime—an eternity from 1983.

Chapter 11
The Unexpected Taunting

Within the next hour, Elizabeth said good-bye to Chad and watched him ride away in the back of a taxicab. She was certain she would never see or hear from him again. The bad memories were already fading deeply into her subconscious. Remarkably, she felt sad and empty after he was gone. She still had one more night in Fort Lauderdale. Unfortunately, Eric, Luke, and Steve still had one more night there as well.

Elizabeth stepped casually out of her doorway and walked toward the beach.

Steve suddenly grabbed her from behind and body-slammed her against the wall. He pinned her, pressed the palms of his hands hard against her shoulders, and peered into her eyes with hatred. "Do you know what we planned to do to you last night? We hate you."

Elizabeth's heart was racing. She couldn't move or speak.

Danielle's boyfriend, George, ran toward them and pulled Steve away.

Elizabeth was too stunned to speak.

"What's wrong with you, man?" George shouted. "Don't you know to never do anything like that to a girl?"

"She's not a girl," Steve remarked with a smirk.

"She looks like a girl to me. What's wrong with you?" George was muscular and strong. He was a football player at the University of South Carolina.

"Where did you come from anyway? Who are you supposed to be, her pimp?" Steve looked all around him.

"What did you call me, asshole?" George clenched his fists and glared at Elizabeth.

A young woman who was working behind the front desk saw the commotion, stepped out of the motel office, and shouted, "What's the problem here? Do I need to kick someone off of this property? Are all of you staying in this motel?"

Elizabeth became especially afraid at that point. The motel only had four names registered for her motel room, and she wasn't listed as a registered guest. She could easily be kicked off the property with nowhere to go. She would become an easy target for Chad's friends if that happened.

Steve responded, "Kendra, you know me. I've been here all week." He stepped back and held his hands up as he spoke. He looked toward Elizabeth and said, "She's the one you don't want hanging around this place!"

"Are these two people causing problems for you, Steve?" Kendra asked.

George remarked angrily, "Are you serious? Steve slammed her against the wall! She didn't do anything to provoke him. I'm here because I'm standing up for her. Steve's a thug!"

"No I'm not!" Steve shouted. "She provoked me."

"I must have missed that part. You grabbed her from behind."

"Stop this nonsense right now!" Kendra scolded. "Move along now —all of you! If I see any more trouble with any of you, I'll kick you all out of here."

Elizabeth made a concerted effort not to be alone again for the remainder of the trip. She walked toward the beach as Steve walked up to his room.

"Why did he do that to you?" George asked as he walked with Elizabeth.

"I don't know, George," Elizabeth replied with a blank stare. "He's not a nice person. That's all I can tell you." She knew that she could never speak again about Chad and his friends. Everyone expected her to justify their actions in some way. She could never justify their actions. What difference did it make anyway? The memories of their cruel ways were gradually fading into her subconscious again. She barely knew their names, but knew she needed to stay as far away from them as possible for the remainder of this trip.

After a couple of hours on the beach with Molly, Lacey and Danielle, Elizabeth needed to go to the restroom. She decided it was safe to walk across the street to her motel room. As she reached the breezeway, Eric approached her from behind.

"Do you know what we planned to do to you last night?" he whispered coldly.

Elizabeth stopped and stared at him. She didn't want to walk back to the beach. She didn't want to walk to her motel room with Eric. She didn't want to attract the attention of any motel employees. She felt polarized.

Eric continued, "Four guys went to a strip club last night. What did you expect? We planned to mutilate you when we were done. Do you know that? Chad wanted to be sure you never have children." He stared at her coldly with hardened eyes. "I doubt you'd ever walk again if we'd gotten to you. You'd be better off dead. But if you survived, you could always turn it into a positive and participate in the Paralympics," he smirked.

Elizabeth was in survival mode. She had nowhere to turn. She visualized herself in South Carolina, far away from these cruel men. Eric continued to taunt her with vivid details about their plans the night before, as if he were enjoying himself. A crowd of people shuffled past, and Elizabeth slipped away with them. She remained in her locked motel room for the next hour.

For the remainder of the trip, Elizabeth was sure to stay by someone's side, anyone's side. She felt very alone in a crowded place. Her only consolation was that it was temporary. She didn't know those dangerous men, and she didn't want to know anything more about them. She was clearly their only target. No one else seemed to be in danger. If she could simply get out of there safely, she would never see any of them again.

Chapter 12
The Reunion

Six Years Later - Fall, 1989

Following the traumatic spring break trip back in 1983, Elizabeth had very little contact with Rebecca or Sandy. But she spent the next two years living in a house off-campus with several other girls from that same trip, and their friendships developed. By 1989, that bizarre trip to Fort Lauderdale had long ago faded deeply into Elizabeth's subconscious. Elizabeth also met Nick Reed during her senior year of college – and by 1989, they had already been dating for several years.

Molly Hendrix had majored in political science while at the University of South Carolina, and accepted a job in Washington DC shortly after graduation. She had been living there for several years before accepting a job that would soon require her to move away to Kuala Lumpur, Malaysia. She had recently accepted the new position to work in the United States embassy.

During the fall of 1989, Elizabeth planned a weekend trip to visit Molly before she moved away from Washington to Southeast Asia. Lacey and Danielle also went along on the trip. Caroline, who had transferred to the University of South Carolina during her junior year, joined them as well. Molly, Lacey and Danielle had all been with Elizabeth on the spring break trip to Fort Lauderdale back in 1983. Caroline, however, had not.

On a crisp fall Saturday morning, Elizabeth and her friends

toured the Washington Monument and the National Mall. Later that same day, Molly commented, "I've narrowed dinner plans down to a couple of restaurants that I think you'll all like. The first has been around for a long time. They serve all types of food, but are best known for fabulous steaks. It's a little farther away from my apartment than the second choice, which is a newer restaurant. The newer one is also known for great steaks. They've been advertising on the radio and are all the rage around here lately. Both restaurants are expensive, but if we're planning to go out for a nice meal, we'll need to spend a few bucks."

Everyone agreed on the newer one. Molly called to make the reservation, but the restaurant was closed for a private party until nine. Molly made a reservation for nine fifteen.

They spent the afternoon shopping around Georgetown before returning to Molly's apartment to get ready for dinner. Exhausted from shopping and touring, they took a cab to a bar near the restaurant. After enjoying a bottle of wine and chatting about old times, they entered the restaurant promptly at nine fifteen.

Upon entering the doorway, Elizabeth noticed that a large partition separated them from the main dining area where the private party was still being held. They were seated near the front door and ordered appetizers and drinks. A short time after being seated, the atmosphere became much more festive. Lights dimmed, and disco music blasted throughout the room. The partition was pulled open, and a hundred new faces joined everyone else in the lively atmosphere.

Drinks were generously being poured around the room, and the dance floor was soon filled. After several songs had played, Elizabeth felt a tap on her shoulder. When she turned around, a tall, lean man with strawberry blonde hair asked if she wanted to dance. Elizabeth asked her friends if they cared if she danced with him.

"Of course. Go ahead and dance. We know you love to dance," Molly remarked.

Elizabeth joined the young man on the dance floor. As they danced together, he tried to ask her a question, but she had difficulty hearing him in the loud room. Elizabeth was dating Nick seriously, and she had no interest in pursuing this young man beyond the dance floor. After a couple of dances, they returned to their tables.

The night continued through dessert and additional drinks. Molly and Lacey danced with two young men from the private party. Midnight was approaching, and the restaurant was about to close.

As the crowd thinned, Elizabeth, Lacey, Molly, Danielle, and Caroline discussed whether they should return home or venture to another bar.

***

At a nearby table, Eric Johnson and Luke Madison were having a similar discussion. The private party that evening was held in honor of Eric's father. Ronald Reagan had recently appointed Eric's father to a powerful position. The economy was booming, and the nation felt a strong sense of American pride.

"I'm getting ready to call it a night, Luke," Eric said. "Anything we do after this magnificent event will be anticlimactic." He peered over Luke's shoulder and nodded toward five young ladies seated at a table near the front door. "You danced with one of those girls over there, didn't you? Do they look familiar to you?"

"I'm not sure," Luke replied.

"I think we both know them. If we don't actually know them, we've met them. Take another look. This is such a small world!"

Luke stared across the room intently.

Eric continued, "I have a photographic memory. It's dark in here. That's the only reason I'm just now figuring it out." He stormed across the room.

Luke followed Eric toward the table, but he decided to continue walking out the front door.

Molly arose from the table and went to the restroom as Eric approached them.

Eric stood at the end of the table and asked, "Did you girls go to Fort Lauderdale a few years ago on spring break?"

"Yes, as a matter of fact, we did," Danielle answered enthusiastically.

"I knew it! I remember you! My friends and I stayed at the same motel," Eric exclaimed as he stared across the table at everyone. "Is Sandy here with you?"

Lacey answered, "No, but I stay in touch with her. We both live in New York."

"That's right! She was a fashion major, wasn't she? She had planned to transfer to a fashion design school that was closer to New York City, right? How's she doing?"

Lacey was perplexed and answered, "No. You must have her mixed up with someone else. Sandy was never a fashion major. She moved back to New York after her sophomore year to attend a community college."

"Hmm, that's interesting. Why did she transfer to a community college?"

Lacey didn't want to embarrass Sandy. "She needed to work on her grade point average. She's still working on that."

"What? She told us she had a 4.0!"

Danielle and Lacey giggled. "You surely have her mixed up with somebody else. She wasn't the studious type."

Eric asked, "What about her friend? Is Rebecca here with you?"

Lacey and Danielle looked at each other and replied, "When were they ever good friends? Oh! They may have hung out together on that trip. We lost track of Rebecca. She dropped out of school and moved away. Quite frankly, we hope she's still alive."

"Good God! Why?" Eric gasped.

"She just had a few bad habits. We really liked her...don't get us wrong...but we hope she straightens out her life. That's all," Lacey answered uncomfortably.

Eric didn't immediately recognize Elizabeth. She was wearing a fitted dress with a scoop neck, long sleeves, and it was above the knee in length. A sash across her back allowed the waist to be adjusted. A small circular opening exposed half of her back.

"I love your dress. We noticed it earlier from across the room," Eric smiled as he gazed deeper into her eyes. His jaw dropped when he recognized her. His smile disappeared.

Elizabeth didn't immediately recognize Eric. He was thinner and had lost some of his hair. "Thank you. I heard you mention Fort Lauderdale. Were you one of the guys with Chad Patterson?" At that point, she recalled Chad as a kind, distinguished gentleman.

Eric's voice rose and his demeanor turned angry. "What in the hell is she doing here with all of you?" He stepped back and pointed toward her, glaring at the others before turning back toward Elizabeth, "That's how you remember me - the guy with Chad Patterson?"

"He's the one I got to know on that trip," Elizabeth responded.

"That's right! And he was engaged on that trip! You went after a guy who was engaged, didn't you?"

"He didn't tell me he was engaged. I didn't know…"

Eric interrupted, "…He's married now and has two kids. In fact, he was supposed to be here tonight, but he couldn't get away from his family. Are you stalking me—or did you come here to stalk Chad? You danced with Luke!" Eric looked around the table. "Why the hell is she here with all of you?"

"We're friends. What the hell is wrong with you? She's the one who planned this whole weekend. If not for her, we wouldn't all be here together. She's our social coordinator," Danielle answered.

Eric became angry. "She orchestrated this trip, huh? That's no surprise! We checked through the partition to see who was sitting out here. You knew exactly how to find us, didn't you, Elizabeth? You fooled us all, didn't you?"

Elizabeth's heart sank in disbelief. She was slowly beginning to remember how delusional and dangerous Eric and his friends were. The fire in his eyes and his irrational conclusions were familiar. She knew she couldn't reason with him.

Eric shouted, "She's here in Washington this weekend for one reason only! You're all pawns! She lured you here because of me! Don't allow her to use you anymore, ladies. She knew I would be here because our party was public knowledge. My dad was being honored tonight!"

Elizabeth attempted to reply, "That's not true. I don't even remember your name or who your father is. I didn't even recognize you when you came over to our table."

"But you somehow got Luke to dance with you, didn't you? He'll be so mad when I tell him about this. You were flirting with both of us from across the room, staring at us, wearing that dress."

"No, I wasn't. You're delusional. He came over to our table and asked me to dance." She looked around at everyone in disbelief. "I didn't even have a conversation with that guy when I danced with him. There was no flirting."

Eric leaned down and whispered, "Chad taught me how easily we can manipulate everyone around you. We can turn anyone against you. Do you realize that? We know just enough about you and your weaknesses to make this work in our favor. Now watch me in action." Eric stood up proudly and announced, "She wanted me in Fort Lauderdale, but she couldn't have me. And now she's managed to track me down here in Washington—and she's using all of you to make it happen." He looked around the table. "My dad is famous, and she's nothing more than a fame chaser! You say you don't remember me? It was only a few years ago. Hey, Elizabeth, are you still a theater major? You see, I'm really intelligent. I don't forget."

"I changed my major to journalism after that trip."

"You were never a theater major! You only claimed to be to try to impress us. You were lying."

"That's not true. You're wrong on so many levels right now." Elizabeth looked around the table and saw the look on everyone's faces. "You can't possibly be falling for this? I didn't choose this restaurant. Don't you remember that Molly is the one who told us about this restaurant?"

Molly had not yet returned to the table.

Eric leaned down and whispered, "I'm a better actor than you'll ever be." He stood upright and proclaimed loudly, "I just graduated from law school. Thank you very much. I have a famous father, and a wonderful world out there waiting for me!" He pointed toward the door. "Good night, ladies. My best advice to all of you is to stay away from her." He stared at Elizabeth with hatred in his eyes.

A bad memory sparked in Elizabeth's brain when she spontaneously remarked, "You're a rapist."

"No, I'm not! We never raped you! You're a liar!"

"You *planned* to rape me...you almost raped me...maybe I would have enjoyed it." Elizabeth's eyes widened, and she covered her lips. She was shocked that these words had somehow formed and sounded from her own lips!

At that point, she had no recollection of Chad's hypnosis. He had told her in Fort Lauderdale that if the subject of the rape plot ever arose within the next twenty-nine years, she would reply: *maybe I would have enjoyed it.*

"Is that right?" Eric replied. "Let me explain something to you. Steve took a huge dump that night. We saved it in a big plastic bag and planned to spread it all over your little body that night. It was meant to be a symbolic gesture. You would have gotten exactly what you deserved. Do you think you would have enjoyed that? Let me tell you something else. If you ever track me down anywhere again, you'll get exactly what you deserve. And I promise that you won't enjoy it!"

Elizabeth was afraid of Eric and fully understood his dangerous capabilities. She never would have enjoyed being attacked. Her conscious mind was fully aware of this, but she couldn't explain her odd response to anyone.

Eric danced toward the door while singing the words to "The Entertainer." He joyfully sang, "Now the curtain is going up/the entertainer is taking a bow/does his dance step and sings his song/even gets all the audience to sing along!" He stopped at the door, skipped and clicked his heels before taking a deep bow. He turned and swung open the door before stepping outside into the darkness.

Everyone at the table with Elizabeth clapped, laughed, and waved good-bye to him.

Elizabeth was suddenly on the defensive. The music stopped, and the room was silent. The lights were turned on, and the waiter came over to their table. "You don't ever want to get on that guy's bad side."

"She's already on his bad side," Danielle responded.

"What did you do to him?" the waiter asked.

Elizabeth had no reply, but the question felt familiar. She couldn't comprehend Eric's deep level of hatred toward her. He had threatened her life. She was afraid of him, but she didn't know him. The only thing she knew was that he was a friend of Chad Patterson's—and they had nearly tortured and murdered her in Florida.

"Did you really lure all of us to this restaurant to meet him?" Danielle asked.

The waiter raised his eyebrows and walked away. "I told the general manager we shouldn't have opened this restaurant to the public during a private party!"

Elizabeth replied to Danielle, "Of course we're not eating at this restaurant because of him. How can any of you possibly believe that? We've all been friends for years. I'm dating Nick. That makes no sense. That guy who just left here is not a good person. Can't you see that?"

"He seems nice. This is all too much of a coincidence," Danielle said.

Elizabeth was astonished with everyone's reactions. "You met him for less than five minutes. You've known me for years. I'm telling you that I did not follow him here. I don't know him. Why are you falling for his lies? Molly picked this restaurant. We all picked it because it was the closest one to her apartment. Molly picked this restaurant!"

Danielle looked around the table. "When Molly gets back to the table, don't tell her about any of this. She'll be hurt. We came here to visit Molly—not to track down a famous guy in a restaurant."

"There is no reason for her to be hurt!" Elizabeth reassured everyone.

Lacey whispered into Elizabeth's ear. "I slightly remember what those guys had planned to do to you in Fort Lauderdale, but you never talk about it. One of those guys called your roommate and threatened you after we got back to South Carolina. You mentioned it to me after we got back to the dorm, but it was a brief conversation."

"I keep blocking it out for some reason. I really have a hard time remembering it happened at all. I hardly remember that guy. I don't know him."

Lacey answered, "It was traumatic, I guess. That's probably why you're blocking it out of your mind. I don't believe you came here looking for that guy, but some of this doesn't make any sense. You must admit that. You shouldn't have said you would have enjoyed it."

Elizabeth couldn't explain why she had uttered those words. It made no sense to her either. It felt horrid. "I planned this trip so that we could all get together and visit Molly before she moves. This trip has absolutely nothing to do with that horrible guy. He's not a nice guy. Why can't you see that?"

"He's not nice to you," Lacey answered.

Molly returned to the table, and the subject of Eric was suddenly dropped. They all decided to go to another bar.

Elizabeth was again shamed and stunned into silence. She said very little for the remainder of the evening. As they walked out the door and onto the sidewalk, she saw flashes of light and heard humming around her head. The memory of Eric Johnson's visit to their table in 1989 immediately faded deeply into her subconscious—until 2012. That specific memory wasn't allowed to return into her conscious mind until March of 2012.

Chapter 13
The Fiery Explosions

Two years later - 1991

Elizabeth received a phone call from her mother. "Something terrible happened to your father today. He's going to be okay though, eventually."

Elizabeth was startled. "What happened?"

"He was in a fiery explosion at work. His face and chest are covered in second-degree burns."

"Oh God! How did that happen?"

"Evidently, two of his coworkers were afraid to put two pieces of equipment together. They asked him for advice. When he tried to help and put the two pieces together, it caused an explosion. That's the best way I can describe it in layman's terms. He was injured the worst. The other two men were standing behind him, and they were slightly injured too. He looks like a monster, but everybody seems to think he'll be okay. Luckily, he has a high tolerance for pain."

"What's he going to do now? Do I need to come there?"

Elizabeth lived a few hours away. Her job had required her to move there, and she was working on her master's degree.

Elizabeth knew how much her father loved his job. She knew this accident wouldn't stop him from working again. She also knew that he would never accept disability for two reasons. First of all, he was adamantly opposed to frivolous government handouts.

And secondly, he would have done anything in his power to stay employed. He was a creature of habit. The idea of not being able to get up and go to work every day would have been a fate almost as bad as death.

Elizabeth's mother continued, "He's still planning to go to work every day until he heals. That's not what people normally do, but this is his preference. He doesn't want to alter his routine. There's an onsite physician who'll keep his wounds and bandages clean and updated. I'll have to drive him back and forth to work for a while."

Michael Green, Elizabeth's father, didn't know at the time of the accident that this would be the beginning of his long and brutal journey with Eric Johnson, a lawyer in Washington. Michael was naïve enough to believe that life was fair and that the details of his accident would eventually come to light. He thought it would all work itself out in the end - but he was very wrong.

One month later, Michael's wounds were gradually healing. He would be scarred on his face and chest, but not nearly as badly as originally expected. Everyone was pleased with the healing process. Everything was working out fine. The other two employees were also healing.

Michael talked with a couple of family members who worked in the insurance industry. One of them explained to Michael that he should consider asking for the maximum amount of compensation from any type of monetary settlement. "Ask for more than the standard amount. Everyone does," Michael was lucky to be alive.

When the day finally came to file for a settlement, Michael took the advice to heart. He asked for more than the standard amount, even though it didn't feel quite right. He didn't consider it a handout. He had been through a horrible ordeal, and he would continue working. The cause of the accident would soon come to light, and he could help them get answers for better safety procedures.

❊❊❊

One month later, Eric Johnson sat at his desk in Washington and skimmed through paperwork. Someone down in South Carolina was asking for too much money after a work accident. He noticed the name of the injured party, and couldn't believe what he was reading. The man's last name was Green, and he lived in Elizabeth Green's hometown. Could this injured party be a relative of the prostitute who had stalked him in Washington? He wanted to find out.

Eric picked up the phone and called his assistant. "Can you please check into something for me? Can you please find out if Michael Green has a daughter or a family member by the name of Elizabeth? I desperately need to know."

Russ immediately began a string of phone calls to Chem-Solutions in South Carolina. He found out that Michael Green did indeed have a daughter named Elizabeth. She lived in Raleigh.

"From this point forward, I'm handling this case personally. Nobody else is touching this one, got it?" Eric shouted.

"I've got it," Russ answered.

Eric was fuming with rage. He now had a new opportunity to destroy the Green family! Elizabeth had treated his best friend horribly in Fort Lauderdale. She treated Chad like trash, but she was the trash! He would make sure everyone knew it. She had later stalked him in Washington, and it was time for her to be exposed.

Eric and his friends had planned to teach her a lesson in Fort Lauderdale, but she had eluded them. He thanked God for his second chance to teach the Green family a lesson! He could kill two birds with one stone—and destroy both of them.

Chapter 14
The Ongoing Delusion

Eric Johnson was certain that Michael Green was a money-hungry man who had caused his own accident. He also concluded that Michael Green had done a terrible job raising his menace of a daughter. It was time for him to pay. Michael Green was making the world a horrible place in the same way that Elizabeth was making the world a horrible place.

Eric's delusion about the Green family was spiraling out of control. He slammed his fist on his desk!

Russ rushed in to see what was wrong. "Is everything all right?"

"This case is personal!" Eric shouted.

"Okay," Russ backed out of Eric's office, softly shutting the door.

Eric picked up the phone and called the human resources department at Chem-Solutions. "Can you please schedule a meeting for me? I'll travel down to South Carolina. I want to meet the key players in the Michael Green case. I can meet any time next week. I'll make it work."

Eric called information and asked for Elizabeth Green's phone number in Raleigh. He tried calling her for several days before finally reaching her at home.

"Hello, is this Elizabeth Green?" Eric asked.

"Yes, this is Elizabeth Green."

"Congratulations! You've just won a brand-new thirty-two-inch television!"

Elizabeth immediately sensed a scam. She didn't watch much television anyway. She was too busy working and going to school at night to complete her master's degree. She was also planning a wedding with Nick. She had too much on her plate to watch television.

"How exactly did I supposedly win this new television?" she asked. "What's the catch?"

"Are you always this pleasant?" Eric asked coldly.

Elizabeth knew something wasn't quite right. "Answer the question. How did I become the lucky winner today?"

"Lucky? Oh, the television - yes! You were randomly selected from a database. We want people like you to try our new product. It's all the rage! You'll love it! All I need is your social security number, and we'll ship this beautiful new television right out to you."

Elizabeth laughed. "You're not getting my social security number. Sorry, I'll have to pass on this good fortune today. Thanks anyway. Good-bye." She hung up, and the phone immediately rang again.

"Elizabeth, why would you pass on this amazing opportunity? What if I throw in a brand-new stereo system?"

"No!"

"Why don't you want this stuff?"

"Because I already have a stereo system—and I don't ever watch television. And quite frankly, I sense a scam here. Nothing in life is free! Nothing comes this easy! You're not getting my social security number, not today—not ever!"

"You're crazy for turning this down!" Eric shouted.

"Are you calling me from a prison cell? Because if you're not, that's where you belong! Don't ever call me again! You're not getting my damn social security number!" She slammed down the phone. Her heart was racing.

Eric Johnson wasn't easily defeated. He needed another way to destroy Elizabeth. He called Luke Madison. "I need a favor. I'll pay you back. I promise."

"What is it?"

"Do you remember that girl we met in Fort Lauderdale, the hooker who stalked me a few years later in Washington?"

"Of course I remember her," Luke answered.

"You're not going to believe this, but her dad is trying to get a whole bunch of money from a bogus work accident. I'm planning to destroy him—and I'll destroy her in the process. I'm killing two birds with one stone, but I need your help."

"That's crazy! How can I help?" Luke asked.

"You've still got family down in New Orleans, right?" Eric asked.

"Yes."

"I want you to testify in a deposition that you saw Elizabeth turning tricks on Bourbon Street. You were down there visiting family, and you recognized her from Fort Lauderdale."

"You want me to lie?"

"It's not a lie when you know it's the truth. We know that she did that. We know that she worked on Bourbon Street. You go down there anyway to visit family, don't you? This is perfect for you."

"But I never saw her down there. That part would be a lie," Luke replied, shaking his head.

"Luke, Chad would help me if he could. I've already asked him. But he's got a young family at home. England is too far away. Will you at least think about it?"

"I'll think about it."

Chapter 15
The False Accusations

The following week, Michael Green and several other Chem-Solutions employees met with Eric Johnson in Columbia, South Carolina. Eric had tried to do his own background research on Elizabeth's current lifestyle, but he kept hitting roadblocks along the way.

As they sat around the table, Eric introduced himself with enthusiastic charm and charisma. He told everyone how he had clumsily walked through the office and bumped into a pile of books on the floor, which caused him to fall on a desk. Everything on the desktop scattered around and fell on the floor. His knees were sore from bumping into everything. He shared his debacle with dramatic flair. Everyone in the room was laughing hysterically at the image.

"I feel like a real stooge right now. Anyway, that's how my day started. Why don't we go around the room and introduce ourselves?"

Eric knew that by openly humbling himself in such a charming, humanistic way, he could win the hearts and minds of everyone in the room. It worked, and everyone introduced themselves.

When Michael Green spoke, Eric's demeanor immediately changed. "Why don't you tell us how you caused that accident? Go ahead. Admit it."

Michael Green was a humble quiet man. It had never occurred

to him that he could be accused of causing the accident. His face lost all color. His mouth dropped open.

Everyone was stunned by Eric's remark. "You're way out of line. Nobody here thinks he caused that accident," one of his coworkers insisted.

"Oh. That's because he's a fraud, just like his daughter. Hey, Michael, do you know I met your daughter in Florida? She was working as a prostitute down there," he said simply with a cold calculated stare. "Then she stalked me a few years later in Washington. She was all over me in a restaurant. She once claimed that she was a theater major in school, but she's really just a very good actress. She's a fraud—just like you."

Michael was stunned. He had expected to discuss the cause of the accident and the extent of his injuries. "Are you sure you're talking about the right person? My daughter graduated from the University of South Carolina a few years ago."

"Her name is Elizabeth Green, right?"

"Yes."

"Yep, I'm referring to your daughter the prostitute. She's the one I know."

Michael arose from the table and walked out of the room. The meeting was over before it ever began. Two coworkers followed him out to the hallway.

The physician remained in the room with Eric Johnson. "I treated him through all of this. He doesn't strike me as someone who would have purposely caused such a horrible accident. He has permanent scars. He's lucky to be alive."

"I think he's got all of you fooled. You'll have to prove me wrong," Eric remarked before rising from his chair and storming out of the room.

Chapter 16
The Ongoing Destruction

Elizabeth traveled to her hometown the following weekend. She wanted to continue making wedding plans with her mother. She had been dating Nick for several years and they were engaged to be married.

On Saturday afternoon, she found herself alone with her father for a moment.

He approached her calmly and asked, "Do you know a guy by the name of Eric Johnson? He's a lawyer."

Elizabeth thought for a moment. The name sounded vaguely familiar. "I'm not sure. How would I know him?"

"You're not sure?"

Elizabeth thought further. "I honestly don't know anybody by that name, not that I can recall."

"He's a lawyer, and he's from one of the most powerful families in this country. He says he knows you."

"How does he know me? I should remember somebody like that."

Elizabeth's father replied matter-of-factly, "He said he met you in Florida. He said you were down there working as a prostitute."

Elizabeth's jaw dropped. She wasn't sure whether to laugh or cry. "That's impossible! You know me better than that. I could never do that." Elizabeth's chest tightened. The thought of discussing anything sexual with her father was demeaning. The conversation was degrading and humiliating and wrong. She felt short of breath.

"He said you stalked him in Washington too," Elizabeth's father continued. "That's where he lives."

"I've never stalked anybody. This is insane. This is way out of line." Her memories were slowly returning but they were vague at first. "I ran into a guy in a restaurant in Washington who accused me of stalking him, but I hardly know him. He's dangerous. Oh goodness. Now I remember. He nearly raped me in Fort Lauderdale." She felt humiliated as the words and the memories began to flow.

"He nearly raped you, but he didn't? You don't need to bring that up. He'll call you a liar for sure." Elizabeth's father sat in the room with the same quiet, calm demeanor that he always displayed. "He's accusing you of being a prostitute. You're accusing him of being a rapist. This is getting ugly. Well, I understand how it feels to be on the receiving end of an outrageous false accusation. He's accusing me of causing that accident at work. Do you think I'm capable of that?"

"Of course I don't think you're capable of that. The thought never crossed my mind."

"Well, I'm disgusted by all of this. I don't care about the money anymore. It's not worth it. I should have never listened to anybody's advice. I should have followed my own instinct. Now that lawyer will say or do anything to destroy both of us." Michael Green got up and walked out of the room.

Elizabeth saw a flash of light and heard humming. The conversation immediately faded deeply into her subconscious.

Chapter 17
The Wedding Reception

August 1992

Elizabeth threw her bouquet high into the air. A couple of single girls fought for it before one of them eventually wrestled it away from the others.

Elizabeth laughed at their struggle as she walked away.

A tall dark young man walked up behind her and whispered, "You have a tiny waist."

Elizabeth turned around and smiled at him.

"You're not letting that body go, are you?" he continued, "It's the only thing you've got going for you."

Elizabeth's smile immediately disappeared.

"That's an ugly dress. I hate your dress," Eric taunted. "Now I feel much better about complimenting your dress in Washington. Ha! And I get to do this on your wedding day. Lucky me!"

"Who are you?"

"I'm a friend of Robert's," Eric answered.

"Who is Robert?" Elizabeth asked.

"Oh, I thought your husband's name was Robert. That's not his name?" Eric stopped and looked around. He seemed perplexed.

"My husband's name is Nick," she replied with a stern look.

"Oh, thank you for telling me. I'm a friend of Nick's. I've been telling everybody here that I'm a friend of Robert's. Oops! Yes, I'm a friend of Nick's."

"You're not a friend of Nick's! You don't even know his name. Who are you?"

Eric leaned down and spoke deeply, "You stalked me in Washington. Now I'm stalking you. Do you know who I am yet?" He stared at her intently.

Elizabeth's jaw dropped. "I didn't stalk you. Why would I stalk you? You're one of those rapists from Fort Lauderdale, aren't you? How did you find me here? Get out! You're a rapist!"

Elizabeth's father-in-law saw the commotion and stormed toward them.

Eric shouted, "How does it feel to be stalked? It doesn't feel very good, does it?"

"I didn't stalk you! I just happened to be out in that same restaurant! You're insane! Get out!"

Nick's father came upon them and inquired, "Do you know this guy?"

"Not really. He needs to leave right now!" Her heart was racing.

John Reed put his hand on Eric's shoulder. "I noticed you earlier. I sensed something wasn't quite right with you. I'm asking you to leave here right now please!"

"Do you know who I am?" Eric asked defiantly.

"I know you're not an invited guest, and that's all that really matters. And if you don't leave right now, I'll have you arrested for trespassing!"

Eric motioned to Russ across the room.

Russ put down his drink, stepped away from the doorway, and followed Eric to the parking lot.

Chapter 18
The Royal Pain

Seven Years later - April 1999

Elizabeth's mother had been the eldest of six children. Elizabeth therefore had many cousins living throughout the United States, but most lived in North and South Carolina. Others were much farther away. One cousin, Meghan, had recently moved to England.

Meghan lived in Leamington Spa with her husband and newborn daughter. She had met Donald many years earlier in South Carolina. They had fallen in love and gotten married while living there. His job eventually required both of them to move to England. They had their first child while living abroad.

During the spring of 1999, Elizabeth visited Meghan. She flew there with her mother and two of her mother's sisters, including Meghan's mother. They spent the first few days in London visiting popular tourist sites. A few days later, they took a train to the Isle of Wight and spent several days there. They spent the last few days of their trip in the central part of England with Meghan.

During one of the last days of the trip, they visited Stratford-upon-Avon, William Shakespeare's birthplace, and strolled along the cobblestone streets touring the sites. They stopped for a late lunch and dined outside at a small café.

Meghan mentioned that it was the last Monday of the month, which meant that a group of psychiatric professionals were having a meeting in one of the nearby buildings. The bells would chime at three o'clock, and they would all venture outside to a café for tea and crumpets. The group met monthly, and they were known to discuss ongoing needs of the royal family. Meghan also mentioned that many of them were affiliated with Oxford University, which immediately sparked Elizabeth's subconscious.

Elizabeth remarked unwittingly, "I met a guy a very long time ago who was affiliated with psychiatry—and possibly Oxford University. I think he may have planned to work in psychiatry over here. I can't help but wonder if he's affiliated with that group."

"A list of their names is posted in the lobby of that bell tower over there. We can walk over and check it out if you'd like. I need to stretch my legs anyway. They won't be taking their break until three o'clock." Meghan replied.

As they strolled up a hill toward the bell tower, Meghan remarked, "Oh, the bells are chiming. That means they're getting out early today."

A group of men and women scattered outdoors from a nearby building. They were walking toward Meghan and Elizabeth.

Meghan asked, "What's his name, that guy you know?"

Elizabeth realized that she hadn't thought of his name in many years. She didn't feel as though she knew him at all. The memory of him was extremely vague. "His name was Chad Patterson," she answered. It felt odd to say his name aloud.

A gray-haired gentleman, who was slightly overweight, walked past them at that precise moment. He quickly turned his head toward them. He stopped and stared at Elizabeth with widened eyes and mouth.

"Well, that must be him," Meghan giggled.

The man cried out, "No, it can't be! Wait right here!" He pointed toward Elizabeth, lunged forward and grabbed her wrist, "Don't go anywhere! I'll be right back." He turned back around and continued walking and talking with the group, but kept glancing back at Elizabeth.

"Was that him?" Meghan asked.

"That guy doesn't look anything like him," Elizabeth replied. Her memory of Chad Patterson was extremely vague.

"I think that's him. He recognized you. How long has it been since you last saw him?" Meghan asked.

"I was in college, back in the eighties, on a spring break trip in Florida. It's been sixteen years since I've seen him. He didn't look anything like that. He was smaller, and his hair wasn't gray."

"Well, he's probably changed in the last sixteen years, especially if he's had children, don't you think? People tend to change after a decade and a half." Meghan continued, "Look at how much I've changed since I had my first child." She stepped back and stared at Elizabeth closely. "But you haven't changed a whole lot, Elizabeth. I think it's because you don't have kids. That's probably why that guy immediately recognized you. And I suppose you really got his attention when you said his name lout loud."

"This is crazy. I'm in a small town thousands of miles away from home. Good God, I'm in England for Christ's sake. This can't be possible."

"Well, it's clearly possible. He's walking back toward us right now. He looks mad," Meghan observed. "I need to go to the restroom. There's one in the bell tower. I'll look at the list of names while I'm in there." She turned away from Elizabeth and walked toward the bell tower.

Elizabeth turned around. Chad was walking quickly toward her with a stern look on his face.

"Don't go anywhere! Stay right there. Don't move!" Chad shouted.

Elizabeth was trying to remember their encounter from 1983, but she couldn't recall many details. She only remembered him as a kind young gentleman. She had no idea why he was angry.

"What in the hell are you doing here? You're looking for me, aren't you?" Chad demanded. He stopped, scratched his head and candidly remarked, "Naturally I'd see you here in this place." He spread his arms apart and held his hands high in the air. "All the world's a stage to you, isn't it?"

"I'm here on a family trip, a vacation." Elizabeth was stunned at his reaction.

"So where's your family?" He looked around. "You said my name specifically. I heard you say my name!"

Elizabeth regretted ever mentioning his name, but it was too late.

Chad exhaled. "Actually, I'm glad you're here. I have a few things that I'd like to say to you. Where did she go, that lady who was with you? Who was that?"

"She's my cousin, and she went to the restroom. She's the reason I'm in here in England. My visit here has absolutely nothing to do with you."

"Let me tell you something. I'm glad she stepped away because I don't want her to hear this first part. You made a fool out of me, didn't you? I was so depressed after I left Fort Lauderdale. I convinced myself that you were the one who got away. I convinced myself that I had blown my future with you because of my nasty temper. I thought I had made the biggest mistake in my life by misreading you, threatening you, and letting you go. I felt guilty for how I treated you. I actually thought about you on my wedding day. I talked to my dad about you before walking down the aisle." Chad shook his head in disbelief. "I wondered if I was making a terrible mistake by marrying someone else. Thank God my dad talked some sense into me. You keep making a fool out of me!"

Elizabeth was startled. "Chad, this is really hard for me to believe. You never seemed seriously interested in me in that way. This is coming out of nowhere. Anyway, everything worked out for the best…are you still married?" She could barely remember Chad. She felt no physical attraction or heartfelt reaction to his words. She felt nothing but shock and disbelief.

"Oh, don't let your ego get too worked up, honey. I'm happily married with children. I'm glad I got to tell you that part while nobody else was listening. And now I'm disgusted and angry that I ever took you seriously! Yes, you're right. Everything keeps working out for the best." He laughed. "It's really fun to build you up before knocking you right back down! It got so bad for me at one point that I contemplated suicide—not for what I did, but for what I *almost* did. I felt horribly guilty about it. I had to get therapy because I couldn't talk to anyone else about it. Do you know what my therapist told me?"

"What did your therapist tell you?"

"He told me that the best thing I could do was to call you and apologize for my actions—for scaring you the way I did. He told me that those two words, *I'm sorry,* would be the most powerful form of healing for both of us." Chad stared at Elizabeth, but she didn't respond. "I actually picked up the phone years ago and tried to call you several times. I wanted to apologize, but I was too scared. I found your phone number, but I hung up every time before you answered."

"I would have accepted your apology." Elizabeth was still struggling to remember the details of what Chad had done.

Chad continued, "None of it felt quite right. I felt like a fraud. You see, this is why I'm not a therapist, even though I work in a similar field. When I went to that therapist, I could never tell him the whole story. I know exactly how this works. People never tell a therapist their whole story. They hide little things. I never told him that I really *wanted* to kill you—and that I *would have* really killed you if I'd had the chance. I never told him that I actually did call you a few days after that trip…do you remember that phone call I made? You weren't there. Before I started feeling guilty and sad, I threatened you again—after I got back home—through your roommate…did she tell you? I told your roommate to leave you a message that I was coming after you in South Carolina! And now… this is incredible! I didn't have to come after you! Here you are! You came here instead - many years later and thousands of miles away! It's too bad we're in a public place right now. I'm so mad at you..."

Elizabeth's memories were slowly returning, but they were vague. She interrupted, "…I do remember that, Chad, and I need to go now." She couldn't comprehend what may have caused him to transition from wanting to apologize at one point – to this anger that he was displaying today. But she clearly understood that he was a danger to her. She started to walk away.

"You're not getting away that easily!" He touched her shoulder.

Elizabeth stared at him, but the memories weren't returning fast enough.

"This is incredible. I had to seek therapy. Meanwhile, you can hardly remember what happened in Fort Lauderdale? What would have happened if I had called you to apologize? How would you have responded? Wait. Don't tell me! You would have asked why I was apologizing to you in the first place." He laughed in disgust. "I'm glad I didn't apologize. I'm angry that we didn't get to gang-rape you because you deserved it, and we would have easily gotten away with it. You needed to learn a lesson. You still do! Hey, what's your cousin's name?"

"Meghan."

"Thanks for telling me that. She's coming back from the bell tower. Her timing is perfect. I can have some fun now," he whispered. "Now watch me in action. Do you remember how clever I am?" He suddenly stood upright and shouted, "What did you just say to me, Elizabeth? Ahh! You want me to divorce my wife and marry you? And that's why you're here in England?" He stopped and glared at Elizabeth. "Well, the answer is no! I'll never leave my wife for you! You're nothing but trash! Do you understand? You're trash!" He smirked at Elizabeth and looked at Meghan.

Elizabeth didn't take him seriously, and was somewhat amused. She was thousands of miles away from home. What difference did it make if Chad tried to embarrass her? He was playing a mind game, and she refused to play along. She waved toward Meghan to keep her distance before turning back to Chad. "That was good, Chad. You're a very talented actor, very theatrical. All the world's a stage to *you,* but Meghan knows me better than that. I've known her my whole life. She knows that we just stumbled upon you out here. Seeing you here is nothing more than a very bizarre coincidence."

"You're a liar. This is no coincidence."

"I'm here visiting Meghan with my family. There's nothing more to tell you. This is a female family vacation."

"You keep saying *family*. Where's the rest of your family?"

"My mother and two aunts are down there at the bottom of the hill waiting for us to get back to them. We need to go now." Elizabeth looked toward Meghan and nodded. "I'm very happily married. I hope you can stay happily married too. Your little charade was very entertaining, but it didn't bother me."

Chad shouted, "You're a liar! You're nothing but a trashy liar!"

"You really aren't bothering me with your mind games and silly theatrics," Elizabeth replied. "I live thousands of miles from here. I don't know any of these people. You're the one making a fool of yourself right now."

"I don't know any of these people either. And I don't live here either—not thousands of miles but about a hundred miles. Anyway, your cousin is standing right over there. You'll need to explain this to her, won't you? You told me she was your cousin?"

"Yes, she's my cousin. She knows better than to believe your silly charade. Weren't you just in a meeting with some of these people?"

"They're not out here anymore. Don't you pay attention to anything? They went into one of those cafés. You should know by now that I'm fully capable of turning anyone and everyone against you, including your very own cousin. Do you understand who you're dealing with here?" He leaned closer and whispered, "Don't you remember what we planned to do to you in Fort Lauderdale? We'd still do that to you today or tomorrow if we got the chance. A penis is a weapon, my dear, but it's much more fun to use than a gun or a knife."

A woman overheard his last remark as she walked past them and responded with a shocked look.

Chad quickly covered for himself and continued, speaking with a British accent, "And I say this to you because many are oblivious to the true nature of this horrific crime, or the motivation within those men who are capable of committing it. Rape is typically motivated by hate and power and oftentimes revenge. Outsiders typically view it solely as a sex crime."

The woman nodded and continued walking.

"Did you see how I just did that? I killed two birds with one stone. That woman believes I was having an intellectual discussion with you about the psychology of rape." He laughed. "At the same time, you got to hear how much I hate you and want to hurt you. You know, it really is a good thing that we're standing out here in the open. Otherwise, you'd never make it back home," he whispered.

Elizabeth saw a flash of light and heard humming. The memories of 1983 began to flood her brain. It had been sixteen years, but the memories crashed into her mind. "Chad, I understand how dangerous you were at the end of that spring break trip." She started to walk away.

Chad reached his arm around her waist, pulled her closer toward him and taunted sarcastically, "Yes, it was so horrible that you passed out at one point, didn't you?" He gazed down into her eyes, "Well, that was surely an act. You didn't remember any of it at all until I reminded you today. And to top it all off, you came thousands of miles here to see me, didn't you?"

"No, of course I didn't. Those bad memories have been blocked for some reason." She stepped back. Her memories were returning faster, and they were becoming more vivid. "And they've been blocked for a very specific reason, haven't they, Chad? Don't you remember what you did before you left? You did something specifically to help me block out those bad memories."

Chad's face turned pale. "What are you talking about? Oh, you're talking about that silly little hypnosis thing that I did?" He laughed and paused for a moment. "I forgot about that. I never took that seriously. I didn't know what in the hell I was doing. That was just something I read in a textbook when I was twenty years old. I did it so that I could rape your mind—since I didn't get to rape your body. And you allowed me do that to you. I don't believe it really worked. You couldn't possibly be traumatized. You stalked me here today—the same way you stalked Eric in Washington!"

"Excuse me? Who is Eric?"

"Oh, there you go again, pretending like you don't remember. I was worried about you. I was worried about myself until 1989. That's when everything changed. You chased down Eric at that restaurant in Washington! When you couldn't have me, you went after him, didn't you? We figured out who you really are!"

Elizabeth was getting dizzy again. She realized that she was forgetting everything about these dangerous men, but she had no control over her memory loss. She wondered if she would forget about this encounter too! It was very concerning. The world was getting smaller and smaller, and the horrible coincidences with these men were surmounting - beyond human comprehension.

Chad's words seemed faint and distant, almost echoing, as he continued. "That worked out really well for Eric in the end. He put your dad in his place a few years later. He may not have ever known who your dad was if he hadn't seen you in that restaurant in Washington."

"What are you talking about? What does my dad have to do with any of this?"

"It doesn't really matter. You got Eric back, didn't you? You had a big fancy wedding. He showed up, thinking he could ruin your big day, but he got kicked out of there and nearly arrested. I can't believe you pulled that one off. How'd you do that to him? You're a fraud. Your wedding was bigger than my wedding. And you're still married?"

"Yes, of course. I'm happily married." Elizabeth heard humming in her head and saw sparks of light. Every memory with these horrid men was being erased from her mind. She couldn't escape them—not even when she was thousands of miles away from home! She knew that Chad had done something to her brain. "You blocked these memories for a very specific time period, didn't you?"

"Possibly," he said softly.

"Do you know how long these memories will stay blocked? I'm not only blocking out the 1983 memories; I'm also blocking out the

Washington experience and my wedding-crasher experience...and what happened with my dad?"

"You're insane, aren't you?"

"You're making me insane. Dear God, this means that I'll block out this memory too!" She stared at Chad. "Didn't you set a time limit on this?"

Chad was quiet for a brief moment. "Twenty-nine years."

Elizabeth was awestruck. "I don't claim to understand this entirely, but my guess is that all of these memories, including today, will return at the same time, won't they? That will be—"

"It will be 2012, Elizabeth. We scheduled it for March of 2012. And you expect me to believe that you stumbled across Eric in Washington in the same way that you're coincidentally crossing my path today in England?"

"I don't care what you believe, Chad, but that's exactly what's happening. Good-bye." She turned and walked away.

"Tell your dad that he'll never get any of that money—not as long as he's dealing with Eric! He hates your whole family!"

Elizabeth didn't understand his comment and continued walking toward Meghan.

Meghan remarked, "That was just some guy you met on a spring break trip, huh? That conversation looked much more intense than some guy you met on spring break."

"Meghan, he's crazy and dangerous."

"He's one of the most prominent people in this country."

"I don't care. He's crazy and dangerous."

"Then why did you want to see him?"

"I didn't! I thought we were going to look at a list of names on a wall. I didn't expect to see him here. And I certainly didn't remember how dangerous he was."

"He's dangerous because he thinks you were stalking him," Meghan answered.

"I didn't expect to see him here today! In fact, I wish I had never mentioned his name. You said two words that sparked my memory of him—Oxford and psychiatrist. What are the odds that he would be here today? In a flash, he was standing right in front of us. This is unbelievable!"

Elizabeth heard humming and saw flashes of light. She realized that the memory of this experience was about to fade, and she didn't know how to keep it intact. "We need to get back down the hill. We've been gone a while. They may think something has happened to us."

Chapter 19
The Game Is Still On

Several Years later - Fall, 2008

Elizabeth and Nick were looking forward to a weekend trip to Maryland. The occasion was for work and pleasure—a college football game. It was to be held at an elite university outside of Washington. Elizabeth and Nick had been planning the trip for quite a while. The weekend was to be held with a large group of friends and major donors affiliated with the university where Nick was employed.

On Thursday, they drove five hours to the small historic town. They checked into a hotel for a good night's rest.

Elizabeth spent the following day shopping and touring the campus while Nick played golf. It was a gorgeous crisp fall day. Later that evening, they dined at an exquisite Italian restaurant. The trip was everything they had imagined and more.

On Saturday morning, a bus transported Elizabeth and Nick, along with thirty additional people, to the football stadium. The kickoff was scheduled for noon. Nick had access to the private suites inside the stadium. The people on the bus were divided into two groups. The first group was allowed access to the private suite during the first half of the game. The second group was allowed access during the second half.

At the stadium, everyone was greeted with a warm welcome and private passes. The first group took the elevator up to the private suite. Elizabeth and Nick were in charge of making sure the first group was comfortable. The large suite had plenty of tables, plush chairs, and private bathrooms. A large open window overlooked the stadium.

Everyone was soon partaking in the delightful cuisine and drinks that were bestowed upon them. Bloody Marys, mimosas, and screwdrivers were poured. Muffins, croissants, bagels, sandwich meats, and fruit were plentiful.

The stadium was soon filled with more than sixty thousand roaring fans. The game was tied at halftime. Elizabeth and Nick were scheduled to watch the second half in a different private suite on the opposite side of the stadium. Friends who lived in the area had invited them. The second suite was even larger than the first one and was filled with fans of both teams.

Nick immediately left for the other side of the stadium when half time began. Elizabeth stayed behind and straightened up to prepare for the second group of guests with the wife of one of Nick's coworkers. Martha and Elizabeth only needed five more minutes to ensure that the suite was presentable for the second group.

Martha and her husband, Kevin, had lived and worked at this particular local university for many years. Kevin had coached football here before eventually moving into athletic administration. Therefore, Martha was familiar with the stadium, the university, as well as the town. She knew many people who supported the opposing team.

After Martha and Elizabeth were finished straightening the private suite, they stepped outside into a quiet hallway. Elizabeth was planning to meet Nick in the larger suite on the opposite side of the stadium.

As soon as they stepped into the hallway, a tall man from the opposing team spotted them and remarked in a jovial manner, "Hey, it looks like we're being invaded by the enemy!" He stared across at them as he moved toward the elevator. "That quarterback you guys have is really talented. He'll be in the pros for sure." He suddenly stopped and stared at Elizabeth for a moment before turning and walking rapidly towards her. "Hey, you look familiar. How do I know you?"

"I have a common face," Elizabeth laughed.

Within seconds, his jaw dropped. "Not again! Not you again! And you don't age! How is it that you always look exactly the same? What kind of facial cream do you use?"

"Oil of Olay. It's cheap, but it does the trick!" As those words flowed from Elizabeth's mouth, she was awestruck. Her response felt vain and silly. She couldn't believe she had actually said it. Her subconscious was already responding to Eric Johnson. Her subconscious was already responding to the hypnosis – to respond like a prostitute.

Eric smirked, "It's cheap, but it does the trick? Naturally you'd say that. How did you two riffraff women get up here? You have nothing to do with our school."

Martha answered, "Our husbands work for the other school. How do you know this guy, Elizabeth?"

"I don't know him, Martha." She stared at him again. "Is it possible that you have me mixed up with someone else? How do I know you?"

Eric was annoyed. "I'm calling security! You two need to leave this stadium right now!"

Martha laughed. "You go right ahead! I know the head of security personally. Tell him I said hello."

Eric stopped and stared at her. "Martha? Is that you? Why are you dressed like that?"

"Well, if you know me, then you also know that Kevin and I are here today with the opposing team, right? That's where Kevin works now. This sort of thing happens occasionally in our industry."

"I'm sorry Martha, but you should never associate yourself with this tramp!" He glared at Elizabeth and sarcastically asked, "How's your dad?"

"He passed away last year," Elizabeth answered.

"Oh, I'm so sorry to hear that." His response was cold and

insincere. "Excuse us for a moment," he nodded to Martha as he grabbed Elizabeth's arm and pulled her toward the elevator.

Elizabeth jerked her arm away from him. Her heart was pounding. "I'm not leaving here with you! I'm going to meet my husband right now."

"Your husband? He works for the other school, doesn't he? Where is he now?" Eric looked around the hallway.

"I'm going to meet him."

"Certainly you know who I am. Do you remember what I'm capable of doing to you?"

The memory of his face finally emerged when she looked deeper into his cold dark eyes. "Oh my God! You're one of the rapists. You're one of those guys from Fort Lauderdale! I didn't recognize you without your hair." She tried to dash away from him.

He let go of her arm, shook his head, and laughed. "Fort Lauderdale? We are so far past that now!"

"Well, I'm not!" Elizabeth gasped. She began walking away toward the suite. "I need to meet my husband now."

He grabbed her arm again, "Wait a minute! It can't be! This is getting better and better!" He stared at her from head to toe.

Elizabeth's heart was racing. She didn't know what he meant.

"Turn around!" He lifted her arm and twirled her around, trying to look at her back. He was much taller and stronger than Elizabeth. She was like a rag doll to him.

Elizabeth was wearing a fitted thick cotton blend shirt that she had owned for many years. It had long sleeves and was cut above the knee. She wore it with tight leggings and tall leather boots. From the front, it appeared to be a simple long scoop-necked shirt. From the back, it had an adjustable sash at the waist. A small round open area exposed part of her back.

"This is the same dress you were wearing in Washington! You kept that dress for all these years?"

Elizabeth still didn't understand what he meant. "Washington?"

"Don't tell me you don't remember seeing me there! This is getting old! How long ago was that? Was it 1989? This is 2008.

Oh my God! You've had this dress for nineteen years! You wore it here today to impress me, didn't you?"

Elizabeth's heart sank. She visualized Satan laughing at her as though he had personally dressed her that morning. She knew he was right, but it seemed impossible. She typically took her used clothes to Goodwill every year, but she always kept a few timeless, high-quality articles of clothing. This dress was one of those garments she rarely wore. She wore it today because it was the school's color. She kept it in an antique cedar armoire in her guest bedroom and rarely ever considered wearing it. She didn't realize she'd had it for that many years!

Eric was now gasping for breath. "You wore this here today to get my attention, didn't you? This is amazing. Do you know that Chad and Luke were supposed to be here with me today, but they had to cancel at the last minute? We rescheduled for next month. When I see them, they're going to be so mad that you followed me up here!"

Martha came over and asked, "Elizabeth, do you need anything from me?"

Elizabeth used that moment to escape from Eric and walked as fast as she could toward the opposite side of the stadium.

"Where do you think you're going?" Eric shouted.

Elizabeth ignored him and looked back toward Martha. "I need to go meet Nick. Martha, I'll see you after the game!" She picked up her pace and started jogging. She saw flashes of light and heard humming sounds as she passed by a young couple. She gradually slowed down, nodded and smiled at the next group of people she passed. Her heart rate decreased.

Eric asked Martha, "Do you know where she's going? I need to find her. She needs to leave this stadium."

Martha knew where Elizabeth was going, but she chose not to tell Eric. She responded that she wasn't sure. She immediately got on the elevator and left Eric standing alone in the quiet hallway.

Eric found a security guard and described Elizabeth to him. "If you see her up here again, she needs to be ejected from this stadium! Do you understand? She's here for no other reason than to stalk me! She's trash!" he declared.

The security guard told Eric that he would search for Elizabeth and eject her if he saw her.

When Elizabeth finally arrived at the suite on the opposite side of the stadium, she found Nick. The memory of her brief encounter with that dangerous man in the hallway was totally gone from her conscious mind, but it was buried deeply in her subconscious. The second half of the game began in a festive new atmosphere. It was as though the incident with Eric Johnson had never occurred at all.

Chapter 20
The Second Chance

A few weeks later – Fall, 2008

Chad Patterson looked forward to returning to the United States to visit old friends. He flew from London to Washington to reconnect with Eric Johnson and Luke Madison. A mutual friend of theirs was engaged, and a bachelor party was planned for the weekend. They had originally planned to get together for a football game, but Chad changed his plans to come later for the bachelor party instead.

On Friday morning, Eric picked up Chad at the airport. They drove to Eric's home in Maryland, and Chad settled into a guest suite. Eric was married with children, but his home still had plenty of extra space for Chad to stay for the weekend. Eric's wife had prepared a scrumptious lunch for them, and Luke Madison soon joined them. They discussed the American political system and declining stock market. Chad told them that he still hadn't fully recovered from his substantial financial losses after September 11, 2001.

After about an hour of discussing politics and the stock market, Eric said, "I'm glad you're sitting down, Chad. Brace yourself. I have something to tell you, and I think you'll be angry about it."

"What did you do?" Chad said.

"It's not about what I did. It's what someone else did—someone who has caused you tremendous anger in the past."

"Tell me more."

"Do you remember that girl we met down in Florida - Elizabeth?"

"Yes, of course," Chad's face turned pale.

"I saw her again last month," Eric exclaimed.

"What the hell? Where did she track you down this time?"

"At a football game—the same game that you and Luke were originally scheduled to be here for."

Chad cried out, "It may be time to press charges for stalking! I almost came here for that game. Where did you see her?"

"She was standing outside my family's suite!"

"Damn! How did she get up there?"

"I'm not sure, but she claimed—"

Eric's wife entered the room, and they immediately changed the subject. She joined them, and Elizabeth's name was not mentioned again during lunch.

Later that afternoon, several mutual friends joined them at Eric's home for happy hour. Eric had a full bar set up for everyone in his expansive man cave. The guest of honor was Riley Davis.

While drinks were generously being poured, Eric told Chad that he wanted to show him something in his office. As they strolled down the hallway, Eric admitted that he didn't have anything to show Chad. He simply wanted to finish their discussion about Elizabeth in private.

"I have a great idea," Eric said. "God is giving us a second chance!"

Chad smiled. "What exactly do you mean by that?"

"When we met Elizabeth in 1983, remember what we planned to do to her as part of your bachelor party?"

"Yes," Chad replied. "Do you think we could get her to come up here for this bachelor party?"

"Why wouldn't she come here?" Eric answered. "She chased you down thousands of miles away in England, didn't she? And she chased me down here in Washington back in 1989—and then again in Maryland last month! Why would she turn down an open invitation to see us both here together?"

"You're a genius!" Chad shook his head. "Yes, God is indeed giving us a second chance. Have you already started working on this plan?"

"Not yet!" Eric sat down at his desk and began a web search for Elizabeth. He found her address, but he couldn't find her phone number. He called information to get her phone number. The operator told Eric that the residence had two numbers: one number for Nick and a different one for Elizabeth. "Why would she have her own phone number? It certainly makes this easier for us, doesn't it? Watch me in action!"

He called Elizabeth's phone number, but there was no answer. "Should I try this other number?" he asked.

"Yes, of course."

Eric called the second phone number, and Elizabeth answered on the second ring. He asked if he could speak to Elizabeth, and Elizabeth acknowledged herself.

Eric announced into the phone, "I'm calling from a marketing research firm. Can you please answer a few questions for us?"

"Yes, of course!" Elizabeth replied. She and Nick were getting ready to join a few friends for dinner, and Elizabeth was sipping a glass of wine. Since Elizabeth worked in marketing, she liked to participate in market research surveys and political polls. She had an appreciation for their work.

"First of all, are you married?"

"Yes."

"How long have you been married?"

"Sixteen years."

Eric and Chad were both astonished that Elizabeth was still married to the same man, but both believed it must be a façade of a marriage since Elizabeth was chasing them both around the globe.

"What is your annual income?"

Elizabeth replied with their combined annual income, which was considered to be upper-middle class.

"And how much of that do you contribute versus the amount that your husband contributes?"

Elizabeth explained, "In 2008, my income doubled my husband's, but this hasn't been a typical year. We've had years when the opposite occurs, and his income sometimes doubles mine. I work on straight commission. This year has been a very good one for me financially. That's all."

"Are you pro-life or pro-choice?"

"I'm pro-life."

"Are you sure about that?"

"Yes, of course. I've evolved on that subject. I didn't always understand, but I now truly believe that life begins at conception."

"Okay, how much money does your dad make?"

"My dad passed away last year," Elizabeth replied. At age forty-five, she couldn't see the relevance of that question in marketing research.

"Well, when he was alive, how much money did he make?"

"I don't know exactly. He was semiretired for the past several years of his life. Why is that relevant here?"

"I'll explain that to you, but I need for you to call me back. Can you do that? We're only allotted a certain amount of time to do these surveys on this line, and you seem like an excellent candidate to continue this conversation."

"Okay, no problem. I work in marketing and want to help as much as I can. I realize that market research is important."

Eric gave her a public phone number for his law firm, which he programmed to forward directly into his home office. She hung up and immediately called him back.

"Hello, Eric's Marketing Research Firm!" he answered.

"Hello, this is Elizabeth Reed. I was given this number to call to continue with a marketing research survey," Elizabeth replied.

"Oh, thank you for calling me back. Elizabeth, this is Eric Johnson. I'm not a market researcher."

"I'm sorry. This is the number they gave me to call."

"You dialed the right number. That's what I'm telling you, but I'm not a market researcher. Again, this is Eric Johnson. Remember me?"

"No, I'm sorry I don't. What's this about?"

"Elizabeth, I want you to know that I'm getting a divorce. We're having a divorce party! Can you come up here for that?" He winked at Chad.

"A divorce party?"

"Yep, it's all the rage these days! Everyone used to have bachelor parties. Now everyone our age has divorce parties! I'm finally getting a divorce. We're celebrating, and I want to see you!"

"Look, I'm very sorry to hear about your divorce, but I'm not coming up there. And I don't know who you are."

"Elizabeth, please don't put us through this fake memory loss stuff again. I know that you know who I am. I refuse to play this game with you!" Eric responded defiantly.

"Is this some sort of joke? How exactly am I supposed to know you?" Elizabeth asked.

Eric changed the subject to keep the conversation moving forward. "I was driving down your street earlier today and saw you working in your yard." As Eric was talking, he did another web search for Elizabeth's home address. He found a photo of her home and zoomed in. "Oh, you have a pretty house. Anyway, when I was sitting in front of your house earlier today, I noticed something. I really like that vine you have growing over your garage. What is that?"

"It's a jasmine vine," Elizabeth replied. "Thank you."

Eric had succeeded in drawing her back into the conversation. She seemed curious. "We sat in our car and watched you work in your yard today," he continued. If he couldn't get her to drive to Washington, he wanted her to understand what it felt like to be stalked.

"Excuse me? Were you here in town visiting one of my neighbors?"

"No, we weren't visiting any of your neighbors."

"Well, why were you sitting in your car on my street? Were you lost? And if you know us, why didn't you come over to say hello?"

Eric stopped. "Does anything ever bother you? You've got a

strange guy here on the phone telling you that he sat outside of your house watching you work in your yard—and that doesn't bother you in the slightest?"

"Strange guy? Didn't you say you know us? I'm trying to be polite, and I'm trying to figure out who you are!"

"Elizabeth, I'm not a strange guy. I'm Eric Johnson. Can you please drive up here tomorrow night and visit me? We can meet over in Washington. I'm divorced now!"

"We're not coming to Washington this weekend! Come down here and visit us if you'd like," she responded.

"No, the purpose of this call is for you to come here. Surely you're not turning me down, are you?"

"I still don't know who you are." Elizabeth laughed as she sipped her wine. "You're a market researcher who seems to know me and Nick. Your name is Eric Johnson. You were here in town today, but you didn't say a word to us—even though you were on our street. And now, you're back in the Washington area. Quite frankly, this doesn't make any sense at all."

Eric was getting irritated. "Listen closely. I've already told you that I'm not a market researcher. I'm a lawyer. And I only have one special request. Please come up here tomorrow night—and don't wear that same dress that you keep wearing. Wear jeans, a solid white T-shirt, and a black leather jacket. Boots are preferable. Can you do that?"

"We have plans tomorrow night. Please explain how I'm supposed to know you."

Eric tried a different tactic to lure her. "I have a question about that school where your husband works. Did you go to Hawaii for that bowl game a few years ago? Wasn't that game played on the day before Christmas? I always wonder who actually goes to those bowl games in Hawaii."

"Yes, of course we went. It was awesome. Some of our family came along too. We celebrated Christmas in Hawaii. It was amazing—the best Christmas vacation ever!" We all stayed in

Hawaii for a week. In lieu of exchanging Christmas gifts, we spent money on traveling instead."

"Hmm, that sounds nice. Was that your first trip to Hawaii?"

"No, Nick and I went to Hawaii back in 1993 too, the year after we were married. His dad had a convention there, and the whole family was invited. We went to Maui that time. The bowl game was in Honolulu—two totally different places. Each trip was totally different."

Eric stared across the room at Chad. "Chad, when we were in Fort Lauderdale back in 1983, you flew out of there early to go to Hawaii for your dad's convention! She's fantasizing about you!"

Eric shouted at Elizabeth. He was infuriated. "I don't believe you've ever been to Hawaii at all, Elizabeth. You're very good at fantasizing, aren't you?" Eric had had a few drinks. He was beginning to spiral out of control. "Do you remember what we planned to do to you down in Fort Lauderdale back in 1983? Do you still think you would have enjoyed that?" Eric covered the phone and whispered, "In Washington, she said to me, 'Maybe I would have enjoyed it!'"

Chad gasped and slapped his hand on the desk. "Oh my God! It worked! I programmed her to say that! The hypnosis really worked!"

Eric's eyes widened. "What did you just say? That's one of the first reasons I thought she was stalking me—because she said that to me! What exactly did you do?"

Chad placed his finger in front of his lips. "It was supposed to be sort of like an insurance policy for us—in case she ever talked about our rape plot. If I could get her to say those words specifically, nobody would ever take her seriously. I never anticipated that she would actually say those words to you one day, Eric." He dropped his head. "That could also be why she never remembers anything."

Eric shook his finger. "That's a bunch of hocus-pocus, Chad! We'll talk about that later!" He shouted back into the phone, "Elizabeth, I need to explain something to you. It seems pretty clear to me that you stalked me in Washington many years ago. You stalked Chad in England too! And you stalked me again last month at that football game. You're definitely stalking us! And tonight, guess what else you did? You picked up your phone and called me tonight, didn't you?"

"I did that because you told me you were a market researcher..."

Eric interrupted, "It doesn't matter what I told you! I can always say otherwise. You've already given me plenty of ammunition to have you arrested for stalking. I have access to the Secret Service. I can order a preemptive strike against you! You should know by now that we're always ten steps ahead of you! And if you continue stalking us, we'll kill you. Got it?"

"How could I possibly be stalking you? I still don't know who you are! I remember Chad, but I haven't seen him since 1983." Elizabeth saw a flash of light, pressed her back against the wall, and slid to the floor. She was in a daze. Her chest tightened.

"You stalked Chad in England!" Eric shouted.

"Seeing Chad in England was a coincidence. I didn't expect to see him there," she answered slowly.

Eric laughed disgustedly. "Are you trying to tell me that every time we see you all over the globe, it's merely a coincidence? If we get within a five-mile radius of you, there's some sort of magnetic force pulling us toward you? Is that what keeps happening? Zoot! Zoot! What are you—a rape magnet or something?"

Eric and Chad laughed hysterically. Luke entered the room.

Eric decided to have more fun. "Elizabeth "Do you remember Monty Hall?" He placed his hand over the phone and asked Chad and Luke. "Help me with this one, guys."

Chad laughed and held up one finger. He mouthed the word, "Power."

Eric asked Elizabeth, "Do you remember what's behind door number one?"

Elizabeth didn't respond.

"Are you still there, Elizabeth?"

"Yes."

"Power is behind door number one!" Eric looked at Chad. "Well,

Monty ... we don't need any more power. Can you tell me what's behind door number two?"

Chad held up two fingers and mouthed the word *hate*.

"Elizabeth, do you remember what's behind door number two?"

Again, Elizabeth didn't respond.

Eric continued, "Behind door number two is hate! We already have plenty of hate too. We don't need anything behind door number two! We're still waiting for what's behind number three. We're tired of waiting! Are you still there, Elizabeth?"

"I'm here."

"Why aren't you hanging up on us? Anyway, if you're still willing to give us what's behind door number three, we'll have everything we need for our perfect rape!"

Elizabeth screamed, "Why are you calling me after all these years? I thought this ended back in 1983. Chad and I worked through this. I thought he was actually a nice guy—a nice guy who almost did something really horrible."

"Well, Chad has since learned that you've been stalking us. He knows what kind of person you really are. Do you know he's sitting right here in front of me? He's listening to you right now."

"Chad Patterson from Boston is listening to us right now?" Elizabeth asked softly.

Eric, Chad and Luke sat quietly for a moment. They didn't know that Elizabeth's memories of them had a tendency to spark in chronological order, and the memories were always vague and slow to return. Since Elizabeth had first believed that Chad was from Boston, that's exactly how she referenced him in her first vague memory of him.

Eric shouted, "Elizabeth, you saw him in England. That's where he lives. We just mentioned that! Why do you still think he's from Boston? What's wrong with you? He hated you in 1983, and he still hates you today. And by the way, if you had decided to come up here this weekend, we'd prove that you're a stalker. We'd have killed you on sight, and nobody would ever blame us. In fact, if we ever see you again, anywhere, we'll kill you! Got it?"

Elizabeth screamed, "You're psychopaths—all of you!"

"That's right. We're psychopaths, and we're proud of it! Don't ever forget it!"

***

Elizabeth immediately hung up the phone, knowing they could be right. From the outside, anyone could believe the coincidences weren't coincidences. She was awestruck that she kept crossing their paths, yet she could never remember any of the encounters. She had never mentioned it to anyone because she couldn't maintain any of the memories. She considered the danger she was in. She realized the memories were quickly fading from her conscious. She saw a flash of light and heard humming as she sat on the floor with her back against the wall.

Nick tapped her shoulder. "Who was that on the phone?"

"They said they were market researchers at first, but they weren't. They aren't nice people."

"What do you mean?"

"I don't want to talk about it. I can't talk about it. I don't really understand it." She could feel the memories draining from her conscious mind and into her subconscious. She knew it was temporary. She knew she would be okay again in a few minutes.

Nick asked, "Are you going to tell me who that was on the phone?"

"No, I don't really know who they were. They said they were market researchers, but they weren't."

"Okay, let's shake this off. That's why it's never a good idea to respond to those types of phone calls. Why do you do that? We need to go meet our friends for dinner. Are you ready?"

"Yes, let's go."

Elizabeth and Nick walked toward the front door.

Elizabeth saw another flash of light and heard humming. At that precise moment, the memory of the phone conversation was erased from her conscious mind.

Chapter 21
The Virtual Rapist

Two Days Later

It had been a busy weekend for Elizabeth and Nick after the bizarre phone call she received on Friday night. The front door had seemed like a revolving door between social events and errands. On Sunday afternoon, when Elizabeth finally sat down in a recliner to relax for a moment, the phone rang. She considered letting it go to voice mail, but she had already been doing that all weekend.

"Hello."

"Is Elizabeth there?"

"Yes, this is Elizabeth."

"It's about time you answered your phone. I've been trying to call you all weekend," a male voice said.

"I'm sorry. It's been a busy weekend. Most people reach us on our cell phones these days. May I ask whose calling?"

"This is Chad from Boston."

Elizabeth had no recollection of the Friday night call. She and Nick knew a different Chad who was originally from Boston. Elizabeth assumed she was speaking to Chad Lanier. She had performed with him in a community theater play before he moved to Baltimore. He had played the role of her husband in *House of Frankenstein*. He hadn't lost his thick Boston accent while living in North Carolina.

Elizabeth replied, "Well, how have you been, Chad? How's Maryland?"

Chad replied, "I've had a nice weekend here in Maryland, no thanks to you. I have something to say to you, Elizabeth, and don't hang up." He began speaking in a low, seductive voice, describing specific details of an illicit sexual experience. At first, Elizabeth was in denial, thinking that she misunderstood his words. Why would Chad Lanier be calling her from Maryland on a Sunday afternoon and speaking to her in such a disgusting manner?

Nick walked past her, and she tried to keep a straight face. She hadn't seen Chad Lanier in at least five years. He asked her not to hang up, but she considered doing so anyway. On the other hand, she didn't want him to get away with doing this! She felt feisty and wanted to tell Chad Lanier that she was angry about his gumption! He had always been very flirtatious with all females, but this was simply unacceptable! This could not be tolerated, and she wanted him to know it. She held the phone away from her ear and stepped onto the back porch.

When he finally paused, she screamed, "You have a whole lot of nerve, Chad Lanier, calling me here on a Sunday afternoon doing that! You know that I'm in love with my husband!"

Chad Patterson responded, "Well, I suppose that's the right answer—except that I'm not Chad Lanier. This is Chad Patterson. Remember me?"

"Chad Patterson?" Elizabeth gasped. "I only know one Chad Patterson…from Fort Lauderdale – the spring break trip back when I was in college. Why are you calling me? How did you find me? How long ago was that?"

"The Fort Lauderdale trip was back in 1983, but—"

"Dear God! It's been twenty-five years! Wow! It's been a quarter of a century!" Her jaw dropped. "Why are you calling me? I thought you were a gentleman!"

"That was supposed to be phone rape."

"Phone rape? What in the hell is phone rape? I wasn't even

listening to you. When you started talking like that, I held the phone away from my ear!"

"Are you serious?"

"Yes, I'm serious. Why did you do that? Why did you call me after twenty-five years and do that?"

"You keep maneuvering your way out of getting raped, don't you? You maneuvered your way out of a gang bang in 1983 … and then again this weekend … and now I can't even phone rape you."

"Why are you doing this?"

"Why do you always ask that? What sort of reasoning are you looking for? I need to hang up now, but I'll call you right back and explain this to you. I need to clean myself up, but I'll call you right back in five minutes. And if you really want answers, you need to answer the phone when I call you—if you can remember who I am when I call you back."

"I'll answer the phone! And I'll know who you are!"

Elizabeth hung up and breathed in the fresh air of the sunny afternoon. The memory of the phone call started to fade into her subconscious, but the phone quickly rang again.

"Hello."

"You answered on the first ring…"

"…Chad, I'm in shock that you would call me here after twenty-five years."

"Why are you referring to twenty-five years ago? You do understand that we've spoken since then, right?"

"No, we haven't. I haven't thought about you at all since 1983."

Chad scoffed, "I saw you in England. Don't you remember that?"

Elizabeth thought for a moment. "I went to England back in 1999. You saw me there?"

"Yes, I saw you there. By the way, who is Chad Lanier?"

"He's a guy I knew a few years ago. We were in a play together. We played husband and wife. He lived in this area for a while. He's originally from Boston, and now he lives in Maryland."

Chad Patterson was certain that Elizabeth was fantasizing

about him again. He thought she was role-playing for him. "Ah, I see. We're husband and wife now. And what was the name of that play, the one when we played husband and wife?"

"*House of Frankenstein*."

"Now that's appropriate," Chad laughed. "That comedy was set in a castle in Europe. Is that your way of telling me that you recall seeing me in England when you were there in 1999?"

Chad did a web search for Chad Lanier in North Carolina, Maryland, and Boston. "Wait a minute. I actually may have found him here online. He's a real person, isn't he? He has military experience. He lived in North Carolina, originally from Boston, and now he lives in Maryland!"

"Of course he's a real person. I just explained all of that to you." Elizabeth slid her hand boldly down her face and rubbed her eyes. The vague memory of seeing Chad Patterson on a hillside in England sparked, but she remained silent. She couldn't remember any details about their encounter.

"Elizabeth, are you still there?"

"Yes, I really saw you in England, didn't I?" Her jaw dropped. "How could I have possibly forgotten that? This is crazy. I really saw you in England, didn't I?"

"Of course you saw me in England. Isn't that why you were there? You're still a pretty good actress, aren't you?"

"I was in England with my family. I hardly remember seeing you at all. Did we talk?"

"You can't be serious. Of course we talked. What's wrong with you?"

Elizabeth saw flashes of light and heard humming. She suddenly knew why she couldn't remember the details of their encounter in England. "Chad, don't you remember? You programmed me to forget all of this. That's why I don't remember seeing you. It makes perfect sense. You should know that. You did this! Why else would I forget seeing you in England?"

"You forget everything, Elizabeth."

"No, that's not true! I actually have a pretty good memory—a very good memory! You did something to make me keep blocking this out. And this is temporary, isn't it? We scheduled a specific time for these memories to return, didn't we? Chad, I'll forget about this conversation too, won't I? You of all people should understand that. How much longer do we have before the memories return?"

"I was only twenty years old when we did that. I don't know how it works. I think we talked about suppressing your bad memories for twenty-nine years."

"That's right! It's been twenty-five years already. Oh my God! What's going to happen in four years?"

"I don't know what to tell you about that," Chad answered. "What was your favorite part of England?"

"You're changing the subject, but I'd have to say it was Westminster Abbey."

"Why was Westminster Abbey your favorite part?"

"It was an amazing combination of history and architecture. Kings and queens were buried there hundreds of years before America was even discovered. How did we move on to this subject?"

"Where else did you go in England?"

"We went down to the Isle of Wight and stayed in a nice bed and breakfast."

"What was it like down there?"

"It was a quaint little island; most of the homes had thatched roofs, and the streets were cobblestone."

"What was your favorite part of Isle of Wight?"

"In the middle of town, there was a tropical rain forest…I just remembered something. In Florida, you kept asking me about my favorite things."

"You saw a rain forest in the middle of town? Where was it exactly?"

"It was hidden. We were walking down a street in the middle of town, and there was a doorway. It blended in with all the other storefronts and businesses. When we stepped inside that door, a trail led us through a massive rain forest."

"So what happened exactly? You were just walking down the

street, and you went through the first door? What was inside that first door—maybe a shop selling souvenirs of the royals, souvenirs of power?"

"I didn't buy any souvenirs of the royal family. I don't have much interest in the royal family."

"I see. So what was behind the second door you opened? Was it a shop selling a bunch of cheap stuff, a few souvenirs you hated, perhaps?

"I didn't buy any cheap souvenirs over there," Elizabeth replied.

"I don't blame you. What happened next? You opened the third door and—what do you know? Incredible! The third door you opened was an opening to an enormous tropical rain forest! Did they charge admission at the third door? That little town converted a beautiful natural creation into a commercial product, didn't they?"

Chad meant to prompt Elizabeth to remember his *Let's Make A Deal* antic, but she didn't. She could only remember him as a kind distinguished gentleman, the person she thought he was when she first met him in 1983.

"That's how it happened, yes. We were checking out the shops, and one of the doors opened into a tropical rain forest. We stepped inside and walked all the way through it. At the end, it opened up to the seashore, a beautiful wide beach with large rocks scattered along the shoreline. Huge, white, mountainous peaks protruded from the ocean: The Isle of Wight."

"Elizabeth, do you not remember almost getting raped?" Chad asked impatiently.

"How could you possibly know about that?"

"I was there," he answered matter-of-factly.

"No, you weren't. I was almost raped in 1985. I lived in South Carolina. You weren't there. It was after I met you."

"Are you serious? What happened to you in 1985?"

"Nothing actually happened to me. I wasn't home at the time. I was a senior in college. We lived in an off-campus house with four girls. I was about to graduate, and was out working on my final project. I stayed at Nick's house. We were dating at the time.

A man broke into our home in the middle of the night and raped my roommate's younger sister. He came in through a window. She happened to be sleeping in my room that night because I wasn't there. It was a horrible home invasion. We moved out of that house the next day and never stayed there again."

"She was sleeping in your room? Seriously? Did you invite that man there? Did she get raped because of you, Elizabeth?"

"Of course not! How could you possibly think that? She was raped because of the criminal who broke into our house—not because of me! He's the only one responsible for what happened. I was dating Nick at the time. Those were the days before computers. I had written my final project, but I still needed to type it. I spent the entire night typing it at Nick's house. I was on a very tight deadline, and wanted to go somewhere quiet with no distractions. I also felt an urgent need to get out of our house that night for some reason. I can't explain it. I wasn't comfortable there at all."

"So you weren't raped that time either? Another person was raped instead?"

"Yes. It was awful. And now that you mention it, the police didn't take us much more seriously than you are right now. They assumed it was an isolated case—that he was somebody we invited. I think they thought we were just party girls. The police could have found him sooner if they had taken us more seriously. They should have found him sooner. He turned out to be a serial rapist who was caught about a year later after more home invasions."

"Elizabeth, do you remember that you were almost *killed* another time—before 1985?"

"What are you referring to? I was in a terrible car accident in 1984. How could you possibly know about that?"

"That's not what I'm referring to either. What happened to you in 1984?"

"A man fell asleep at the wheel. We almost had a head-on collision on a four-lane road. He was coming toward me at an angle. I sped up straight ahead, and almost escaped him, but his car veered sideways and slammed into the back of my car. I spun around several times before sliding backward and crashing into a field. My car was totaled, but I wasn't hurt at all."

"Are you serious?"

"Yes. The first miracle is that I survived the car accident. I had to kick open the door to get out. The second miracle is that, when I stepped out of the car, there were live wires all around. I didn't step on any of them. I could have been electrocuted."

"That seriously happened to you in 1984?"

"Yes. That's the closest I've ever come to being killed. It was horrible."

"So in 1983, you were almost killed. Then again in 1984, a car accident almost killed you. And again, later in 1985, you were almost raped in a home invasion? And the last time, someone else happened to be sleeping in your bed?"

"I've never really thought about it that way. I've had a few close calls in my life, I suppose. You're right about 1984 and 1985, but nothing happened to me in 1983."

"Let me ask you a question. When you watch the Natalee Holloway story on the news…you know about that story, right?"

"Yes, of course I know about that story. It's been all over the news for a long time. What year was that—2005? It happened three years ago. Nobody was ever convicted."

"Exactly. Nobody was ever convicted. When you watch that story on the news, do you ever think that same thing could have happened to you?"

"When I watch that story, I think about Natalee Holloway and her family—not about me."

"You look like her. When I see that story, I think about you. You look like her."

"No, I don't!"

"Yes, you do. And I can't believe you've never considered the uncanny comparisons. I think about it every time I see that story on the news."

"What comparisons?"

Chad lowered his voice and said, "Think about it, Elizabeth. We planned to do something really horrible to you in Fort Lauderdale, but you eluded us, didn't you? Don't you remember that conversation we had the next day in your motel room? I told you all about it. We're four powerful guys. One of us is the son of a powerful judge. You're a southern blonde with no power. I would have had to be extradited, which never would have happened. We had the perfect plan. Those guys in Aruba evidently had a perfect plan too. Like you said, there still hasn't been a conviction in that case even though it happened three years ago. Those guys are being protected by a system that takes care of the powerful elite. That same type of system would have protected us back in the eighties, Elizabeth. You should be a missing person right now."

Elizabeth saw flashes of light and heard humming in her head. A vague memory of Chad standing over her in that tiny motel room in Fort Lauderdale entered her mind. "Are you saying that every time you watch that story on the news, you think about what you and your friends almost did to me in Fort Lauderdale?"

"Finally, you're getting it! Yes! That's exactly what I'm saying!" He exclaimed.

Elizabeth cried out, "I suppose you're one of the few people who sees Natalee Holloway's picture and thinks she must have somehow done something to deserve her fate?"

Chad was silent.

Memories began to flood Elizabeth's brain. "Are you still there, Chad? That's how you made me feel. I felt like I deserved it. You and your friends were convinced that I deserved it, weren't you? That's what I'm remembering now. I know how I felt."

"That's not what I think when I watch that story on the news, Elizabeth. Natalee Holloway didn't deserve her fate."

"She didn't deserve it, yet I did? I'm the only person on the planet who deserves that fate, according to you, right?"

Chad didn't respond.

Elizabeth continued, "Van Der Sloot thinks he's invincible now, doesn't he? He'll do it again because he knows he can. But he'll make a mistake somewhere along the way. He's clearly guilty of that crime."

"He's too smart to do it again. The radar is on him," Chad replied.

"A person that evil can't help himself, especially if he feels invincible. He'll do it again," Elizabeth replied defiantly.

"I suppose I shouldn't have made the comparison. Natalee Holloway wasn't working as a prostitute in Aruba, Elizabeth. You were working as a prostitute in Florida."

"No, I wasn't! I was on a spring break trip. What the hell are you talking about? What's wrong with you?"

"Here we go again, Elizabeth. I know that you were working as a prostitute."

"Where did you get that crazy idea? That's disgusting! I could never do that! What's wrong with you? You know me better than that!"

"Sandy told us you were a prostitute. Why would she say that about you?"

"If she told you that, she lied!"

"Elizabeth, after we had sex, you told me to run a tab."

"What did you just say?"

"You told me to run a tab."

"If I said that, it must have been in reference to something else—not sex—or it was a joke or something. I'm not capable of selling my body for sex. That's a fate worse than death! The thought of that is terrifying. I can't imagine it!" She was getting short of breath. Her chest tightened.

"I don't really care if you were a prostitute or not. We had planned to rape you before we found out that you were a prostitute anyway. That revelation was simply a bonus. It made things easier for us. We knew we could do whatever we wanted to you at that point."

"What a horrible thing to say!"

"You did deserve it, Elizabeth. I'm glad you understand that. We needed to teach you a lesson, but you still haven't learned anything, have you? Since then, you've been stalking us. I actually believe you might still be working as a prostitute. You have a vivid imagination."

"You're wrong on so many levels right now!"

"Do you expect us to believe that we've simply had a whole lot of coincidental encounters, Elizabeth? Everywhere we go, there you are! Is the world really that small?"

"What do you mean?" The memories of seeing Chad and Eric over the years were fading in and out of Elizabeth's conscious mind, like a twinkling light.

"You stalked Eric in Washington in 1989! You stalked him again in Maryland at the football game last month! And you stalked me in England! But Eric got you back. He crashed your wedding." Chad laughed. "Unfortunately, his plan backfired. Your father-in-law kicked him out."

"Who came to my wedding?"

"Eric missed the actual wedding because he couldn't find the church. He came to your reception instead. He was planning to make a toast to you, but his plan backfired. Your father-in-law kicked him out. But he got through to your dad, didn't he?"

"My dad? What did he do to my dad?"

"Oh come on now. There's no denying what Eric did to your dad."

"What in the hell did he do to my dad at my wedding reception? That's the only time in my life I ever saw my dad consume alcohol."

"Do you know something? What's happening here reminds me a bit of *Les Miserables*."

"What do you mean?"

"In the beginning of *Les Mis,* a young woman is forced into prostitution. As a result, she gets raped and eventually dies. A father figure, Jean Valjean, is continuously stalked by Javert, who, in the name of law, only sees the world in strict shades of black and white. The two main characters continually cross each other's paths over the course of many years. A wedding eventually got crashed, and the wedding crashers got tossed out of the celebration."

"Chad, I'm having trouble remembering all the details right

now. And I think this phone conversation will fade away as soon as we hang up. Occasionally I understand what's happening. I think this memory loss is temporary."

"Back in 1983, you said you were part of the Baptist church. Are you still active in the Baptist church?"

"I converted to Catholicism."

"Why?"

"Nick is Catholic, and he's very devout. I started going to the Catholic Church in college—before I met him. I was much more comfortable there. We were married at his Catholic Church. Converting to Catholicism seemed like a natural transition after we were married."

Elizabeth felt as though she was in a trance again. Chad was now treating her as a human being again. Her mind converted to viewing him as a kind, distinguished gentleman.

"What's your favorite part of the Catholic Church?" he asked.

"The sign of the cross," Elizabeth replied, but the words made no sense to her. The words formed a response from her lips without her consent. She was mystified. Her favorite part of the church was actually the homily. She loved listening to the weekly message and applying the teachings to her everyday life.

"The sign of the cross?" Chad seemed perplexed. "What is that supposed to mean?"

Elizabeth continued in a trance. "Catholicism does the sign of the cross—physically, I mean. It's a physical way to acknowledge the Holy Trinity—Father, Son, and Holy Spirit. The Baptist church never did that." Elizabeth felt like a puppet. She had never considered any of this before today, but the words were forming against her will.

"Okay. When you pray, what do you pray about?"

"It depends on the individual situation. But I suppose a constant in most of my prayers is for three things: peace, guidance, and wisdom."

Eric and his friends entered the room. "I'm on the phone with Elizabeth. Be quiet!" Chad motioned.

Eric cried out, "Why are you on the phone with her? You said you were going to stay here and take a nap before you travel. How long have you been on the phone with her? We've been gone for two hours. Is she still working as a prostitute? Are you still trying to get her to come here?"

"No! We may have been wrong about some things," Chad replied before speaking into the phone again, "Where are you working now? I thought you'd be a famous actress by now," he said sarcastically.

"I work for a marketing firm."

"Where's your office?"

"It's located in my house."

"You work on commission, don't you? In a nutshell, do you push your products and services on unsuspecting people?"

"Of course not. I'm not pushy. In a nutshell, I help my clients acquire more customers."

"Give me an example of how you do business. Role-play with me."

"No! Today is my day off. That's silly. I'm not doing that."

"Oh, come on now. Please."

"What's the name of your business?" she asked reluctantly.

"I have a zoo."

"You're a zookeeper?"

"Yes."

"Okay, how far away do 80 percent of your current customers travel to visit your zoo?"

"They travel from all over the world to visit my zoo!"

"Okay, that's nice. Do you sell annual passes?"

"Yes, of course."

"Where are most of those people located—the ones who purchase the annual passes?"

"Okay, enough of this. I don't see how asking a bunch of stupid questions can help anybody!"

"In order for me to help someone acquire more customers, I need to know who their potential customers are, and where they're located. We need to go fishing where the fish are biting. But that's fine. I didn't want to do that anyway."

"I don't want to talk to you anymore anyway." Chad suddenly hung up the phone.

Elizabeth saw flashes of light and heard humming. The memory of every conversation that she'd had over the weekend with Chad and Eric was immediately erased from her conscious mind.

Chapter 22
The Prediction Comes True

May 2010

On Sunday, a big news story broke. It caught Elizabeth's attention in a peculiar way, but she wasn't sure why. Joran van der Sloot was accused of fatally stabbing a young woman in his hotel room. It was the fifth anniversary of Natalee Holloway's disappearance; van der Sloot had evidently gotten angry when he discovered the woman searching his computer for clues about Natalee Holloway.

Elizabeth had predicted the day would come, but she wasn't sure why it felt personal. Soon thereafter, the phone rang.

"Hello."

"Have you watched the news today?" a male voice asked.

"Yes, I have. May I ask whose calling?"

"This is Eric Johnson. I'm sure you don't remember me, do you?"

"No, I'm sorry. I don't."

"Of course you don't. The only reason I'm calling is because Chad has been trying to reach you, but every time you answer, he has the international delay. And then you hang up. You must think he's a telemarketer, huh? I suppose you're not taking any more calls from telemarketers?"

"Who is trying to call me?"

"Oh, of course you don't remember," Eric replied. "I'm referring to Chad Patterson, the guy who lives in a castle in England, the one you're stalking. I thought you were stalking me too, but evidently he's the only one you're after. Is that right? Every time you stalk me, it was during a time that he had planned to visit me - but his plans changed."

"Chad Patterson? I only know one Chad Patterson. I met him in Fort Lauderdale a long time ago. I'm not stalking him or anybody else. What in the hell is wrong with you?"

"Stop it, Elizabeth. I'm calling because this is bullshit! Every bit of this is bullshit! First of all, you're nothing like Natalee Holloway. That comparison should have never been made. I don't know why Chad said that, but he was wrong! And we are nothing like Joran van der Sloot either!"

Elizabeth had a vague memory of an earlier discussion of how van der Sloot would someday commit another murder. She felt herself falling into a deep, hypnotic state. She saw flashes of light and heard humming.

"Are you still there, Elizabeth?"

"Yes."

"Did you hear what I said?"

"Yes."

Eric continued, "Secondly, you're a disgrace to the Catholic Church. The sign of the cross is your favorite part of the Catholic Church? What is that supposed to mean? That's the dumbest thing I ever heard!" He paused for a moment. "Unless you were trying to put us in our place about door number three? The number three seems to be a constant through all of this, doesn't it? The sign of the cross ... the Father, Son and Holy Spirit ... the Holy Trinity," Eric said. "We all originally met in 1983. You stayed in room number three." Eric shook his head. "Are you really hypnotized? I felt like I was for a moment there. That was weird."

Elizabeth felt enlightened for a brief moment. Everything Eric described seemed clear, and she fully understood things to be temporary. "You're exactly right," she responded.

"What does that feel like ... if it's true ... to be hypnotized?" Eric asked.

"Hypnotized? Is that what you call this? I have a deeper perspective right now. I'm still blocking out bad memories, and that's what this is really about. But these bad memories keep piling up. Right now, I feel like I'm standing in a tent where all those memories are stored. They're all stored in their own little boxes. We keep adding more boxes. At some point, I'll have to open all these boxes to find out what's inside. I'm not looking forward to that."

"That's weird. Why are you standing in a tent? Why aren't you in a castle?"

"That would be nice, but the reason I'm in a tent is because a tent is temporary and fragile. It will eventually be taken down—and easily so. Occasionally, I'm required to step inside this tent to get a glimpse of what's in here. The boxes are all closed right now. I don't know what's inside any of them. The most remarkable part is that when I step outside the tent, I won't know that the whole tent was ever here at all. Quite frankly, this is the first time I'm seeing all of this with such clarity. When we hang up the phone, I'll have no recollection that this conversation ever happened. This conversation will become a new box inside the tent."

"That's a really nice gig you've got going, Elizabeth, but I'm not buying what you're selling—at least I don't think I am yet."

"I really don't care. I'm not selling anything. You asked me a question, didn't you? I answered."

"Okay, fine. I have something else to say to you. I know that you wrote a nasty letter to my father about me. It was sent to him anonymously, but I know you were the one who sent it! He got it in 2008—not long after the conversation you had with Chad. It compared me to the Javert from *Les Mis*."

Elizabeth was appalled. "You're delusional! I don't know you at all. I don't know your father. I haven't written any anonymous letters to anybody!"

"Elizabeth, stop it. I know you wrote the letter. My dad might start figuring all of this out! I'm really mad at you!" Eric continued. "Anyway, I got my revenge. I wrote a nasty letter to someone about you too." He laughed. "By the way, I hate that job you have."

Elizabeth was disgusted with Eric's delusion and hatred. "I didn't write that letter! You're insane. And I really don't care how you feel about my job, but if you feel so strongly about it, why don't you give me your e-mail address? I have five hundred coworkers. You can tell us all how you feel. We can each reply to you and explain why we enjoy working in the marketing profession."

"Where are all those employees located? You work out of your house, don't you?"

"We're spread out all over the country. Some of us work from home, but most are located in our corporate office."

"Where's your corporate office?"

"It's located in Birmingham, Alabama."

"Well, what do you know? Another coincidence, huh? Birmingham, Alabama is where Natalee Holloway's from!" He slammed down the phone.

Elizabeth saw flashes of light and heard humming. "I need to take Lily for a walk." She grabbed the leash and led Lily out into the fresh spring air.

The memory of the conversation with Eric Johnson in 2010 was temporarily stored away into a tiny box inside of a fragile tent. Two years still remained before the box was scheduled to open.

Chapter 23
The Awakening

Two Years Later - March 3, 2012

Elizabeth awakened in a cold sweat. Even though she kept a dream journal, this particular experience during her slumber felt nothing like any dream she'd ever had before. Someone had reached deeply into her subconscious. The mental picture of him was vivid. Elizabeth considered writing an entry in her dream journal, but decided against it. She wasn't sure if she wanted to remember this dream - but she already knew that she might not have a choice.

Suddenly, there was a knock on the front door downstairs. *Who could possibly be visiting at such an early hour?* It was barely daylight outside.

Nick was sleeping next to her. Quickly slipping into her thick robe, she scurried down the stairs and peeked out the window. A man in his early twenties was standing on the porch. He was smiling. His handsome face was partially covered with designer sunglasses. His thin, tanned, muscular body was dressed for a summer day. He wore navy shorts and a neatly pressed T-shirt.

She stared back at him unknowingly.

He raised the sunglasses over his head, as if to identify himself, and called out her name.

She didn't recognize him. She opened the door slightly and said, "Good morning."

The man smiled and called her name again.

She gradually widened the door open.

He gently pushed the door forward and slipped into the entranceway. The hardwood floor creaked under his flip-flops. He straightened his stance with confidence. Removing his sunglasses, he leaned down and gazed deeply into her eyes. "I'm passing through town and wanted to see how you're doing, Elizabeth. You don't recognize me, do you?" He studied her face for a response.

She tried to smile and answer him, but she was speechless. She was beginning to feel nervous even though he seemed harmless and friendly. There was some comfort in knowing Nick was upstairs.

The man laughed when Elizabeth apologized for not recognizing him. He winked and said, "It's quite all right. It's been a while. You'll figure it out." He looked around the hallway and dining room and said, "You have a nice home."

He was nearly a foot taller than Elizabeth. Her long blonde hair fell over her face as she sheepishly peered up toward her uninvited guest.

He nodded and said, "Have a good day." As he stepped back onto the porch, she felt relieved. She quickly closed the door, locking it behind him. She realized that he hadn't arrived in a car. *How did he get here? Where is he going now? Nick is normally a light sleeper. And why didn't Lily bark or run down the stairs to greet that stranger?*

Elizabeth awakened in a cold sweat. She sat up in the bed and noticed that her robe was still hanging on the bathroom door. Lily and Nick were both asleep in the bed next to her. Elizabeth was stunned to realize she had dreamed it all. It had felt incredibly real—more real than any other dream she had ever had. She chose not to write it down. It felt uncomfortable, and she didn't want to remember it. She rested her head on her pillow and pulled a blanket over her head. Soon, Elizabeth, Nick, and Lily were fast asleep again.

Chapter 24
The Comforting

Two Days Later - March 5, 2012

Elizabeth's father had passed away five years earlier on March 5, 2007. Other than that, this was an ordinary workday. Even though she worked as a consultant for a large marketing firm based out of Birmingham, her personal office was located inside her home in North Carolina. The job required her to travel around the region most days. But unless she was required to go to Birmingham for corporate meetings, she typically returned home at the end of each workday.

On the morning of March 5, 2012, Elizabeth knew that she had a two-hour drive ahead of her to Wilmington. With a big presentation planned for the entire staff of an advertising agency, she was looking forward to it. Elizabeth had not personally met any of the staff members, but she had worked with most of them by phone. They seemed to be a fun group, and she was excited to put all of their faces together with names.

Having worked with the same marketing firm for many years, Elizabeth was accustomed to long drives and meeting new people. She enjoyed it most days, especially when the destinations included beautiful scenery with large bodies of water such as the Atlantic Ocean, Pamlico Sound, or Albemarle Sound. When time allowed, she would schedule walks on the beach or waterfront at the end of the workday before the long drive home. She knew she would do that today on the anniversary of her father's death. It would allow time for reflection. Wrightsville Beach was one her favorite places on earth.

March 5, 2012, was a Monday. Elizabeth didn't typically schedule appointments out of the office on Mondays. They were usually planning days. However, Monday was the only day that all the staff members at the advertising agency would be in the office at the same time. She had no choice but to accommodate their schedules and decided to take full advantage of the situation.

The meeting with the five employees lasted a couple of hours and went well. After the meeting, she ventured to Wrightsville Beach before the two-hour drive home.

Elizabeth drove to Shell Island Resort and easily found a place to park. The beach was quiet even though this was a warm, sunny day. She removed her shoes and jacket, rolled her pants up to her knees, and walked toward the crashing waves and cawing seagulls. The sounds grew louder as she crossed through the path between the tall white sand dunes.

She gazed beyond the broad stretch of sparkling sand to the glistening emerald green water. Bright sunshine sent millions of tiny white shimmering lights down to earth; they were dancing atop the sand and water for as far as she could see. The sand felt comforting, like soft powder underneath her feet and between her toes, but the water was frigid. She strolled toward the point where inlet waters divided Wrightsville Beach from Figure Eight Island. She eventually stopped at the end of Wrightsville Beach and stared across the inlet and marsh to the expansive homes on the edge of Figure Eight Island. One tall home expanded around the curve at the end of the beach. Its windows fully covered the exterior and provided an amazing view in all directions. She wondered if that was the home from *Sleeping with the Enemy*. She knew that a portion of the movie had been filmed in one of those homes. No matter how many times she walked down that stretch of beach, something new always captured her attention—and the views never failed to take her breath away.

Her father had been diagnosed with cancer on December 15, 2006. According to the doctor, he needed to make plans for the next three to six months of his remaining life on earth. The doctor had been optimistic. He died less than three months later.

Elizabeth strolled down the beach, continuing to reflect. Her father had been married to her mother for nearly fifty years, and they battled the cancer together. Elizabeth had spent the last ten days of her father's life at her parents' home even though they lived six hours away in South Carolina. He handled his inevitable fate with dignity and grace. He was a Christian, and he read the Bible daily during that time. He read an additional five books about death and dying after his diagnosis, and finally passed away with a big smile on his face.

Elizabeth and her dad had never been particularly close, especially in their younger years. He had always been quiet and emotionally distant. During his last days on earth, she wanted to be there for her mother. But in doing so, she learned more about her father and was grateful for the opportunity.

Elizabeth continued to reminisce. Her dad never drank alcohol—except for one drink during her wedding reception. Since Michael had watched his own father die from alcoholism, he had never seemed tempted by it. But twenty years ago, on Elizabeth and Nick's wedding day, he gave in to temptation.

Michael had stopped smoking several decades before his death. He exercised daily and made sure to have regular checkups. He even took baby aspirin daily to protect his heart, and he never seemed to have any stress. His demeanor had always been calm and quiet. Yet with all of these precautions, he died from cancer at age sixty-eight. God had evidently decided that it was his time to leave this earth, and it was not a subject for negotiation.

Elizabeth continued to reflect as she strolled down Wrightsville Beach. She gazed down at the shimmering sand below and couldn't believe what she saw. At the tip of her foot was a perfectly shaped round sand dollar. It was so close to her foot that she nearly stepped on it. She understood the miracle of finding a sand dollar that was not cracked or broken into several pieces. Considering the numerous times she had strolled on beaches, she could count on one hand the number of times she had found an unbroken sand dollar. She reached down to pick it up, and was concerned that she might break it simply by touch.

The discovery of this perfect sand dollar was rare, and Elizabeth usually considered it to be a talent. Her father-in-law had possessed that talent. She had walked along the beach with John many times in South Carolina. He knew how to identify the unique way that a section of sand would swirl beneath the wind in shallow waters at the turn of tide. John had kept a tide timer to know when the lowest tide would occur, and it was the best time to find solid sand dollars. John had possessed the uncanny ability to find the hidden treasures during afternoon strolls along the seashore. He had attempted to train Elizabeth on several occasions, but she didn't seem to have the eye for discovering perfect sand dollars like he did. Her father-in-law had explained that finding them in shallow waters at low tide meant there was less likelihood that they would be broken. After washing ashore, people and animals were much more likely to have stepped on them. They were solid and safer in the shallow waters—before drifting onto dry sand. He also taught her how to identify those that were still living, and to toss those back into the ocean.

Today, Elizabeth was walking in warm, dry sand instead of swirling shallow water. This magical sand dollar appeared at her feet in perfect form—and she wasn't even searching for it! The tiny round piece of art was practically smiling at her. It felt like a true miracle. As she continued down the beach with the treasure in her hands, she considered the legend of the sand dollar.

Many believe that the sand dollar represents **the birth and death of Jesus Christ**. When **examined closely,** one will see **four distinct holes that are believed to represent four nail holes: two at the hands and two at the feet of Jesus. A fifth hole in the center is believed to represent a Roman's spear. On one side of the sand dollar, there appears to be an etching of the Easter lily.**

A Christmas poinsettia appears to be etched on the opposite side. Even when broken, the tiny fractures typically resemble small white doves, symbols of peace. The message seems to be that we can seek peace from Jesus Christ, even when we are broken. Elizabeth felt as though God was sending a clear message that He was watching over her on the anniversary of her father's death. She felt comforted as she strolled back to her car.

The tide of Elizabeth's life was turning, but she didn't know it yet. Like the unexpected discovery of the fragile sand dollar, Elizabeth would soon learn that life can also be fragile and unpredictable.

During her journey home, the memory of a recent dream flooded her mind. That mysterious young man remained in her subconscious, but she still had no idea who he could possibly be. The radio blasted the lyrics to an old familiar song by Gino Vannelli: "I am lost living inside myself/ living inside this shell./I am lost somewhere inside my own dream/afraid of what life really means."

Elizabeth eventually pushed the dream from her thoughts and relished in the beauty of the day. She felt grateful during the drive home.

As she carried her new treasure indoors to wash it, she thought about its meaning again. She considered the ongoing significance of the number three. March was the third month of the year. The sand dollar symbolized the Holy Trinity—the Father, Son, and Holy Spirit. A sense of peace and comfort washed over her as she cleaned the sand dollar and stored it on a shelf.

From that point forward, it blended with all the other sand dollars and seashells she had collected over the years.

Chapter 25
The Unraveling

March 2012

As a very happily married woman, Elizabeth couldn't answer her own questions. She had dreamed of a handsome young man at her doorway three weeks earlier and couldn't shake the memory of him. Why couldn't she forget that simple dream—and why should it matter? It had felt incredibly real. Most dreams vanish from our memory within moments after awakening, unless we make a concerted effort to remember them by writing them down, which is precisely why Elizabeth kept a dream journal. She sometimes read back through it and found it comical. Other times, she found hidden messages that seemed to speak to her through her own subconscious. But this time was different. She hadn't recorded any details of the dream. In fact, she *wanted* to forget it. Instead, a nagging sensation felt like a tiny little gremlin in her head, knocking and pleading to escape. *Who was that guy in my dream?* She knew the answer would eventually come if it was meant to be, but tried to block the dream out of her mind.

Finally, on a rain-drenched afternoon three weeks after the dream, the answer suddenly came—at least part of it anyway. Elizabeth considered the number three again. She had met the young man during March! However, that was many years ago. She knew exactly who he was! She felt embarrassed. Why on earth would a happily married woman have a dream about a man she had briefly met nearly thirty years earlier? She occasionally had dreams about people in her past, but she always knew immediately who they were. This time was different.

She had forgotten about Chad. She was about to turn fifty. Could this be the beginning of a midlife crisis? Figuring out his identity felt anticlimactic, but now she hoped to forget about it and move forward.

She went to a cabinet, pulled out an old scrapbook, and skimmed through it. She studied a few photos that had been taken on the beach in Fort Lauderdale. There were volleyball nets scattered around, and she recalled playing volleyball quite often during those lazy days. She noticed a photo with Chad and his friends in the background. The picture had been taken before she actually met him. Chad, who was tan and fit, was wearing the same navy shorts he had been wearing in her dream.

She thought about Chad's thick, brown, wavy, sun-drenched hair, dark brown eyes, and dramatic eyebrows. He had complained because his roommates wouldn't allow him to shave his eyebrows that week because too much hair was being shaved, and their sinks were getting clogged. She laughed as she looked through the faded photographs, astonished at the clarity of details that were flooding her brain. She closed the scrapbook and put it away. *That was another lifetime.*

Elizabeth reflected for a moment. She and Nick didn't have any children, but they stayed busy working, traveling, and giving back to their church and community. Elizabeth also sang in the church choir and occasionally performed with the community theater. She served on several boards for nonprofit organizations. Their extended family members were all located out of town, mostly out of state, and they tried to visit with them as often as possible. Elizabeth and Nick both had strong religious faith. She felt grateful and content during that brief moment of reflection with the realization that life is fleeting and precious. She and Nick had lost three of their parents within the last five years—each with little to no warning. Elizabeth's mother was still alive and was a cancer survivor.

She glimpsed at the binding of the scrapbook before closing the cabinet door. She hadn't looked through those pages in many years, possibly a couple of decades. The contents were old, faded, and beginning to fall apart. She hoped it wasn't symbolic of her life. Approaching fifty, she felt fortunate to be healthy and in pretty good shape. She smiled to think that some of the girls who had been with her on that trip were still her friends today —even though they were scattered throughout the country. Other than a few wrinkles, they all still looked similar to the long ago photographs. She assured herself that the old scrapbook was not symbolic of their lives.

Elizabeth and her friends were planning a reunion trip to the Outer Banks of North Carolina to celebrate their upcoming fiftieth birthdays. Perhaps she would tell them about her silly dream, and they could all laugh and reminisce about that spring break trip.

The mystery was solved—or so she thought. She knew who had appeared in her dream, but she didn't yet understand *why*. Why had the thought of Chad lingered until she could finally realize his identity? She convinced herself that it shouldn't matter. She told herself that it was time to forget about it and move forward.

Chapter 26
The Unspoken

April 2012

As warm water splashed across Elizabeth's face in the shower, time stood still. Warm water trickled down her body and gradually grew colder as forty-five minutes passed. Frigid water and vivid memories of 1983 were overtaking her body and soul. She shuddered as if awakening from a daze that had overpowered her for forty-five minutes. She hadn't thought about any of it in decades, but it was beginning to overtake her thoughts on a daily basis. Elizabeth was reliving 1983 in her mind, and it felt like it was all occurring in the present. The nagging memories were beginning to affect her productivity at work.

During the spring of 1983, Elizabeth had been in the middle of a sophomore slump. Her sophomore year had been a fork in the road. She had insecurities about her future and indecision about her college major. Her high school friends had all been moving in separate directions. And even though she was making new friends in college, it wasn't quite the same. She felt as though she was losing her solid foundation with no clear path ahead either. She had been experiencing an identity crisis, and wasn't close to her mother or father. Her mother had struggled with alcoholism, and her father had always been emotionally distant. It seemed impossible to grow close to anyone during that time. She felt as though she was watching someone else's life unfold in her mind.

A month had passed since her dream. Ever since her realization that the young man was Chad Patterson, specific details of the trip invaded her brain on a daily basis. She would remember a general conversation or event at first, and then more specific details about that conversation or event would soon follow. It was like putting together an enormous puzzle. Every time a new piece was found, it felt as though a new memory was happening again in present tense. The details were vivid and appealed to all of her senses. She could recall specific scents, feelings, and facial expressions.

Elizabeth kept asking herself why it was happening, and she was beginning to understand the level of deception that had occurred all around her during the trip to Fort Lauderdale. She tried to tune out the memories, but was unable to do so.

When the first unpleasant memory about Chad unexpectedly popped into Elizabeth's brain on a beautiful day, it felt like a slap across her face. She had been working quietly at her desk. During a brief pause to gaze out the window and admire the trees blooming in her yard, the world immediately turned dark. She was dazed and confused. The horrible sting of that first memory lingered for an hour. She couldn't be sure what had occurred during that hour. And the memories continued.

Chapter 27
The Ongoing Distractions

April 2012

Elizabeth searched for Chad Patterson on the web. The memory of his face was vivid. She found him immediately. Dr. Chad Patterson was living in a small town outside of London. There was no mistaking those big brown eyes. He still had a full head of wavy hair, but it was gray.

Elizabeth thought, *I survived, but has he killed anyone else and somehow gotten away with it?* She fully understood his capabilities, and she wanted to know more.

Memories of 1983 continued to flood Elizabeth's brain on a daily basis. This was becoming an ongoing distraction in her workplace. She occasionally found herself in a trance as details emerged into her conscious mind. She didn't know how to make it stop. She would sometimes find herself looking at the time with the startled realization that she had no idea what had occurred in the past half hour or so.

One day she had an appointment with a young man who managed a kitchen design store. Jim's specialty was granite countertops. She had developed a good rapport with Jim while working with him on marketing ideas. She eventually invited him to her home to provide an estimate on a renovation project that she and Nick were planning. Elizabeth and Nick eventually hired Jim for their renovation, and he did a fabulous job.

A few weeks later, Elizabeth met Jim at a coffee shop to discuss further marketing ideas for his company. She looked into his eyes and became immediately distracted. He was much younger than Elizabeth, in his twenties, with wavy brown hair and big brown eyes. She suddenly realized that he had a stunning resemblance to Chad Patterson. Her conscious mind couldn't maintain control of what happened next. He continued to speak, but she could no longer hear him. She could only see the face of Chad Patterson in front of her. Jim recognized that Elizabeth was becoming distracted and asked if she was all right. Elizabeth apologized and explained that she had remembered something she needed to do. She needed to leave immediately. She apologized for being rude, but knew that she could never explain what was happening.

They both rose from the table. "We've discussed everything we needed to discuss here anyway," Jim responded. "You can move along now and get that done – whatever it is that you need to do."

They walked toward their cars. Jim told Elizabeth about his weekend plans with his parents in Raleigh.

Elizabeth smiled and nodded, trying to appear engaged. She returned home with a new realization that her memories from 1983 were becoming a genuine problem in her everyday life.

Later that evening, Elizabeth finally told Nick about her memories from 1983. In April of 2012, this is all that she remembered. She explained that she felt lucky to be alive after that trip to Fort Lauderdale during her sophomore year of college, and apologized for being distracted about it lately. It felt like an amazing mental release to confide in Nick. He listened carefully, and was very understanding.

The following week, she met with her direct supervisor. Elizabeth considered Harriett a good friend. Elizabeth needed to explain the distractions that could no longer be avoided.

Elizabeth and Harriett met in a beautiful setting along the marina in New Bern, North Carolina. Elizabeth began by telling Harriett that she didn't understand exactly what was happening to her. She was having vivid memories of something that had occurred in 1983. It had been traumatic, and she had blocked it out of her mind for nearly thirty years.

Elizabeth asked Harriett if she could double check orders and reports for the next little while. She was concerned about mistakes. She was normally very attentive to details.

Elizabeth shared some of the details from 1983, and explained the ongoing distractions as best as she could. Harriett surmised that the memories could be returning because Elizabeth's conscious mind was now strong enough to absorb the mental stress. She was in a secure place with her job, marriage, and social life.

"This too shall pass," Harriett assured her.

It felt very comforting for Elizabeth to get her story out in the open. If anything happened at work, she could now speak about it openly with Harriett. It felt like part of her healing process. She was finally beginning to see the light in an otherwise very dark place in her mind.

Elizabeth realized the healing power of speaking about this. But speaking aloud was only half of the process. The fact that someone else was actually listening and understanding what she had endured was an amazing feeling. It felt as though they were reaching their arms out to pull her from a deep, cold, dark, and lonely tunnel.

A couple of days later, Elizabeth called Molly Hendrix, who now lived in California, and said, "I need to ask you a question. This is going to sound really strange, but I need to know what you remember about that spring break trip to Fort Lauderdale back in 1983."

Molly had a very good memory, and Elizabeth hoped Molly could help validate her memories by filling in some of the details.

"I have a very good reason for asking, which I'll explain, but please tell me what you remember about that trip."

"I remember that Rebecca was out of control. And Lacey's high school friends picked her up and threw her into the swimming pool with all of her clothes on, which was terrible and funny at the same time." Molly laughed. "Danielle fell asleep in the hot tub. Don't you remember? We put an empty beer can under her head to keep her head afloat—so she wouldn't drown. Her head was bobbing up and down in the hot tub!"

They both laughed and reminisced about the trip. "We did some silly things back then, didn't we?" Elizabeth acknowledged.

Elizabeth explained what had almost happened and explained her current situation.

Molly listened emphatically and asked, "Is it possible that you're thinking about this because we're all planning a trip this fall? Or perhaps this could be a premenopausal issue?"

"I don't think this has anything to do with pre-menopause. And we've taken plenty of trips together since 1983. I haven't thought about that trip at all in the past twenty-nine years. And now I can't get it out of my mind."

"I'm not sure what to tell you except to say that those guys are nuts, especially if they thought you were a prostitute. Good God! Thank God you're all right—and they didn't actually harm you physically. Hey, wait a minute. I just remembered something. Everybody thought those guys were distinguished gentlemen. They seemed really refined."

"Yeah, that's what I thought at first too. That's what makes this especially unbelievable. I trusted them. Everyone else did too. That's another reason I had trouble talking about it. It was difficult to get anyone to take me seriously. I remember Chad distinctly, but have no idea who the other three guys are. I'll call you later if I remember anything else. Thanks for your insight, Molly. This conversation was helpful."

As Elizabeth hung up the phone, she heard a very old song on the radio. Dusty Springfield was singing *Windmills of Your Mind.* The lyrics struck a chord with her: "Like a door that keeps revolving in a half-forgotten dream / Or the ripples from a pebble someone tosses in a stream / Like the circles that you find in the windmills of your mind / Like a tunnel that you follow to a tunnel of its own, down a hollow to a cavern where the sun has never shown / Half-remembered names and faces, but do whom do they belong?"

Chapter 28
The Unending

May 2012

Spring was changing into summer. Days were growing longer and warmer. Elizabeth was enjoying the sunshine through her sunroof as she returned home after a long day of work appointments. Her cell phone rang, and she noticed that the caller was unidentified. After years of working in sales, Elizabeth was accustomed to receiving calls from people she didn't know. She had grown comfortable with getting to know people by phone—sometimes without ever meeting them in person.

A male voice spoke, "Hello, Elizabeth?"

"Yes, this is Elizabeth. How can I help you?"

"I'm a friend of your husband. I've been trying to get in touch with him, but I haven't been able to reach him. Can you help?"

"Yes, of course! What can I do to help?"

"I hope you don't mind. I called your home office in Alabama, and they gave me your cell phone. I told them I'd heard you've been working as a call girl from your house—and I wanted to find you."

Elizabeth was startled, but she assumed that he simply had an odd sense of humor. "Good Lord!"

"I'm kidding. I called the phone number that's listed in your name. Your outgoing message gives all callers your cell phone number. You should really be careful about that."

This conversation was taking an odd turn. Since Elizabeth had always worked in sales, she *wanted* people to be able to contact her. She had never considered it to be problematic.

He continued, "I'm trying to plan something, and I need to know if you and your husband will be attending a wedding later this month in your hometown?"

"Well, yes we are. I'm driving right now and don't have my calendar in front of me. Believe it or not, we actually have five weddings to attend between now and July. Whose wedding are you asking about?"

"It's at the end of this month. Someone famous will be attending. Have you not heard about that?"

Elizabeth laughed. "No, I haven't heard about anyone famous coming to a wedding here. But if you're referring to a professional athlete, that's not a novelty to us. It's part of Nick's job to work with professional athletes. We don't think about their notoriety in the same way other people do."

"This won't be a professional athlete. You really haven't heard about this?"

"No, I really haven't heard, but it doesn't matter anyway. That famous person, whoever it is, should be able to attend the wedding as an invited guest. They shouldn't be treated any differently than anyone else." Elizabeth had never been easily star struck. "May I ask whose calling?"

"I'm a friend of your husband."

"Okay, do you have a name? I'll be happy to give Nick a message from you."

"Nick? No, there's no need for that. I'll try to call him again later."

Elizabeth was perplexed. "Do I know you?"

"You and I met a long time ago. My name's Chad. How many people do you know by the name of Chad?"

"I know a few. It's a fairly common name." She briefly considered the coincidence that his name was Chad. This couldn't possibly be Chad Patterson. "Do you have a last name?"

She heard him speaking away from the phone to another person, "I can't do this anymore. She's being professional and polite."

The male voice came back on the line and replied, "You and I danced together once, a very long time ago." There was a click, and he was no longer there.

***

Back in Washington, Luke Madison hung up the phone and said, "I'm sorry. I didn't want to use my real name. And I thought I could get her to reveal something to us if I said my name was Chad. That didn't go very well. I was no help at all."

Eric Johnson replied, "Don't worry about it. You tried. I should have never asked you to do that. I'll call her and find out if she's going to the wedding. What are the chances anyway? Just because she lives in that town doesn't mean that she'll actually be at that wedding. Give me her cell phone number."

***

Elizabeth's phone rang again. It was a private number.

"Hello."

"Hello, Elizabeth. I have a business here in Washington and need to know if you and your company can help me with some marketing ideas."

"Yes, of course. I'll be glad to help you. What type of business do you have?"

"I operate a zoo in Washington."

"You operate a zoo in Washington? I haven't heard about a zoo in Washington. Is it already open?"

"Elizabeth, there is a major national zoo in Washington. How is it possible that you don't know about it?"

"We have a zoo in Washington, North Carolina?"

"Elizabeth, I'm calling you from Washington, DC!"

"Okay, I apologize. I typically work with clients in Washington, *North Carolina*. Excuse me. How did you get my contact name?"

"I called your home office in Birmingham, Alabama."

"I'm surprised they told you to call me about that. I'm driving right now. I'll call you back from my office in about twenty minutes. Do you mind if I get your phone number and call you right back?"

"No, I'll call you back promptly in twenty minutes."

Elizabeth was concerned. After being in sales for many years, she didn't want this contact to get away without getting their name or phone number. "Why don't you let me call you instead? I'll only be a few minutes."

"Elizabeth, I promise that I'll call you back in exactly twenty minutes," Eric answered.

Elizabeth hurried home and carried her briefcase upstairs. By the time she sat down at her desk, the phone rang again.

"How's that for punctuality?" Eric asked.

"Exactly twenty minutes. Perfect. I've been thinking about this. I'd like to do some demographic research around the Washington area and ultimately schedule an appointment to meet with you in Washington." The drive to Washington was about four and a half hours. She needed more details about the industry and area.

"Nope, I want to get all of my information over the phone. There is no reason for you to come here," he replied.

"I'm in no position to give you any immediate details over the telephone at this time. I'll need to do some research if we are planning to discuss marketing for the zoo in Washington."

"How much does marketing cost?"

"It could cost $1,000 to $100,000 or more annually. It depends on your budget and your marketing goals. There's no answer to that question at this time. I need to find out more about your needs and your budget before I can give you an estimate."

"Just tell me how much it's gonna cost!" he demanded.

"I'll be happy to answer that question after I gather some more information."

"What else do you need to know? This whole town is a zoo. It's filled with bears and donkeys and monkeys. We need to train these animals. How do you think you can help us here in Washington?"

Elizabeth laughed. "I don't think I'm the one who can help with that particular problem—and certainly not by phone."

"Elizabeth, Elizabeth. You haven't figured out who I am yet? Come on! I work in Washington, but I don't work in a zoo. Certainly you know who I am!"

"Excuse me?"

"Can you ever remember anything? Good Lord!"

A short silence followed.

"So you aren't in charge of a zoo?"

"I don't have time for this nonsense. Are you planning to attend a wedding in your town at the end of this month? I need to know, and I need to know right now. I don't have any more time to monkey around."

Elizabeth looked at her calendar and replied, "Yes, we are. We're planning to attend a wedding here in town at the end of this month. Is it the same one you're asking about? The bride and groom are Catherine and William. We're also one of the host couples for their post-rehearsal party the night before."

"Great! That's just great! We have another coincidence with you! I knew it!"

"Who is this?"

"You know who I am! You wrote an anonymous letter to my dad, and I'm furious about that. I am so mad at you for that!"

Elizabeth became annoyed. "Excuse me? I have no idea who you are, and I haven't written any anonymous letters to anybody! Tell me who you are!"

"I'm not playing this game with you anymore. My dad is going to be at that wedding. I can't be there to stop you, but I'll find a way to silence you if you plan to say anything to him about me."

"You must have me mixed up with somebody else. I don't know who you are—or who your father is. How could I possibly say anything to him?"

"Yes, you do! Let me ask you a question. If you had a chance to say something—anything at all—to a United States Senator, what exactly would you say?"

"What does that have to do with any of this?"

"Answer the question."

"Okay, if I had the floor in front of any United States Senator at this point in time, I would ask him or her to please help put a stop to Obamacare. We need healthcare reform, but this is not the answer. Our country can't afford it. Small businesses can't afford it."

"It's not Obamacare. It's the Affordable Care Act, but I suppose it's good that his name is attached to it. Okay, we got off track. I don't care what you think about the Affordable Care Act. Why can't you ever remember anything about me?"

Elizabeth answered, "I really don't know who you are, and I don't appreciate your tone or your mind games."

Eric asked Elizabeth to hold on for a moment. He whispered, "Luke, she's still saying she doesn't know who I am."

Elizabeth considered what was happening for a brief moment. This person on the other line kept asking her to *remember* him. And he was being extremely rude. Meanwhile, she had been remembering vivid details about spring break of 1983 lately. It seemed implausible, and she felt somewhat in a daze before finally asking, "What am I supposed to remember? You can't possibly be one of Chad Patterson's friends? Are you one of those guys from Fort Lauderdale back in 1983?"

Eric was startled. "1983? When Ronald Regan was president? Well, that's when all of this started."

Elizabeth's heart started racing. She was numb for a moment before responding, "That's impossible. For the first time in nearly three decades, I'm remembering vivid details from spring break of 1983…and now you just happen to call me to ask about a wedding here in North Carolina? And somehow these two events are connected? How can that possibly be? How did you find me?"

"Oh my God!" Eric shouted. "I'll find another way to take care of you!"

Eric hung up and said, "We can't tell Chad about any of this until after that wedding. I want to enjoy my long weekend in the Caribbean with him and our wives. I don't want to be worried about what's happening at that damn wedding in North Carolina! I need you to go down there and make sure she stays as far away from my dad as possible. I'm still not sure if I believe she's an invited guest. We need to find out for sure."

***

Within a few seconds of hanging up the phone with Eric Johnson, Elizabeth heard humming around her head. She saw a flash of light and had no recollection of the phone calls she'd just received from Eric Johnson and Luke Madison. Since the memories were all returning in chronological order, it wasn't time to remember....not yet.

Chapter 29
Another Wedding Encounter

May 2012

The wedding of Catherine and William was approaching, and it was destined to be a memorable one. The bride and groom were both medical students at Duke University.

Elizabeth and Nick were friends with Catherine's parents and felt happy and excited to be invited. Several weeks earlier, they had received a letter asking them to host a post-rehearsal party. They happily obliged. The party was held in an historic building that had been recently renovated. The wedding was at one of the city's oldest buildings, a Methodist church that had been built in the late 1700s.

While getting ready for the wedding, Elizabeth decided to wear a small diamond necklace that she had had since 2008. While getting ready, the clasp to the diamond necklace wouldn't work properly. She was growing more and more impatient.

Nick shouted, "Come on! It's getting late! We've got to go!"

"Looks like I need your help with this clasp again." Elizabeth handed the necklace to Nick, pulled up her hair, and turned her back to him.

Fumbling with the clasp, Nick said impatiently, "Something's wrong here. This clasp is not working. I think it may be broken. You need to wear a different necklace. We've got to go!"

She chose a glistening crystal cross necklace with a delicate silver chain, and they hurried out to the car. Elizabeth appreciated the idea of wearing a symbol of Christ to a Christian wedding. She decided that her necklace choice worked out for the best.

At the church, all the parking lots were filled. They had to park several blocks away before scurrying toward the church. Hundreds of impeccably dressed guests were listening to a violin, which served as a backdrop to soft whispers, sweet smiles, and nodding guests.

As the ceremony began, a young woman stepped onto the pulpit to sing the most beautiful a cappella rendition of the Lord's Prayer that Elizabeth had ever heard. The soloist sang slowly with strong emotion in every word. Everyone in the room was deeply moved. Elizabeth softly touched the cross around her neck: "Thy will be done on earth as it is in heaven ... deliver us from evil." She listened intently to every word and felt the strong presence of God's love in the room.

As the bride and groom exchanged vows, one of the bridesmaids began to slump forward. Her brother was seated on the front row; he lunged toward her and assisted her to a seat next to him. The wedding never stopped. She remained seated and appeared to feel better as the wedding continued.

The church had cathedral ceilings, and numerous stained-glass windows expanded from front to back. The center aisle stretched between forty rows of pews. The church easily accommodated hundreds of guests.

Catherine and William were a stunning couple. Catherine had flowing, silky auburn hair, bright blue eyes, and a perfect smile. Elizabeth and Nick had never met the groom. William was a handsome man with wavy blonde hair, a big smile, and deep blue eyes. He was from New Orleans.

After the vows, the crowd stood and clapped as the happy couple raced toward the front entrance. The bridesmaids and groomsmen followed, moving to triumphant sounds of the trumpet and organ. The guests filed out of the church row by row, and the triumphant music finally came to an end.

The reception was held in a beautifully renovated equestrian center. The building was large enough to host several events at once, but this particular wedding party was so large that the reception required the full use of the entire facility. The room was filled with people of all ages from all around the country. Elizabeth and Nick mingled separately at the beginning.

Nick found some local guys and struck up a discussion about baseball season. Elizabeth saw the parents of the bridesmaid who had nearly fainted. She asked if everything was all right. Their daughter had low blood sugar and hadn't eaten enough. Stress was involved as well, but she was fine. Elizabeth joined another group of women, and they talked about their upcoming summer plans.

Eventually, everyone gathered together to watch Catherine's father give a toast to the newly married couple. Daniel was proud of the fact that the bride and groom were using their lives to make the world a better place. He knew that the entire room was filled with people who had chosen to do the same with their own lives. He thanked everyone for attending and for influencing both families. He was a happy and proud father.

After a glass of wine and an abundance of small talk, Elizabeth went to the restroom. When she returned to the reception area, she searched for Nick. It had been nearly an hour since she had seen him.

Elizabeth noticed the groom across the room. He was walking straight toward her at a fast pace. She turned around to see if he was coming towards someone else, possibly someone behind her, but he wasn't. He was clearly coming to speak to her. She met him with a smile, reached her hand out to him, and commented on the beautiful ceremony, particularly the singing. "Your wedding day is surely blessed," she added.

William responded coldly, "You actually went to the wedding too? I need for you to leave now."

"Excuse me? What did you say?"

"You weren't welcome at the wedding. And you're certainly not welcome at this reception."

"Why?"

"You weren't invited, and you don't know anybody here."

"Surely you have me mixed up with someone else? Hello, my name is Elizabeth." She extended her hand again, but he didn't acknowledge it. "Actually, I know quite a few people here. We're invited guests on Catherine's side. You know Catherine, your new wife? You do realize that they invited people too, right?"

He nodded.

"We helped host your party last night." Elizabeth and Nick had sent money to host the post-rehearsal party, but they hadn't been able to attend because Nick had to go out of town for work at the last minute. Elizabeth decided not to attend the party alone. None of the host couples were required to do anything to prepare for the party; they simply paid for it.

William replied, "I didn't see you at that party last night."

"We were unable to attend at the last minute, but we didn't want to miss the wedding."

"You keep saying *we*. Who are *we*?"

Elizabeth wanted to be gracious with the groom, but she was getting annoyed. "I'm here with Nick, my husband. We've been married for twenty years. He's a good friend of your new father-in-law. Maybe you should go ask your father-in-law if we're invited to this wedding."

William looked puzzled. "Where's your husband now?"

"I'm looking for him."

"Sure you are. Well, he can stay. You must leave now."

"Is there a hidden camera in here somewhere?" She laughed, but William wasn't amused.

He responded with an angry stare.

"With all due respect, I'm not leaving here without my husband. We've been married for twenty years. We came together in one car, and we'll leave together in one car. I'll find him and we'll leave, but I promise I'll find out why you're doing this to us. This makes no sense at all."

William responded, "Excuse me for a moment. Don't leave yet. I'll be right back. We're not done here."

Elizabeth loved weddings, which were meant to be happy celebrations of love. Something was going terribly wrong at this one, and she didn't have a clue as to what it could be. She was no longer in the mood for small talk. Her head was spinning—partially from the glass of wine and partially from her strange encounter with the groom. She walked toward the bar and searched for Nick. She couldn't find him anywhere.

***

On the opposite side of the room, William sat down next to his cousin. "Luke, she says she's been married for twenty years to a man who is a friend of my new father-in-law. I didn't realize she was that old. She doesn't look that old. Is she lying?"

"What difference does it make how old she is? She's a wedding crasher!" Luke replied.

"I guess her age doesn't really matter. It's just that I thought you were referring to a girl who was my age, not your age. She's almost as old as my parents. Even when I was talking to her, I thought she was closer to my age. I'm a little confused. That's all. I need for you to tell me more about why I'm doing this."

"She's here for one reason only: to cause a scene with Senator Johnson. Senator Johnson's son crashed her wedding a long time ago. She's here for revenge. Eric warned me that she would crash this wedding, seek out his father, and cause a scene!"

William asked, "Why did Eric crash her wedding? Wasn't that twenty years ago?"

"It doesn't matter how long ago it was! He crashed her wedding because she deserved it. And now she's crashing this wedding tonight so she can get to Senator Johnson and retaliate against Eric. That's all I know. If she figures out who I am, I'll have to deal with her too. You need to get her out of here as quickly as possible. You're the groom. Therefore, you have the power to make it happen. Do you want her to spoil your wedding day? Do you want to spoil Catherine's wedding day? Don't you love her?"

"Okay, I can try to make that lady leave, but can you think of something that will make her *want* to leave? That might work better. If she's embarrassed or humiliated because of something that I know about her, it might work without causing a scene."

"Ask her about the time she lived in New Orleans. She worked on Bourbon Street as a prostitute. She doesn't think anybody knows about that. Or ask about her father. The first thing she'll say is that he passed away. Don't let that stop you. Pressure her to talk about him. When she realizes that you know intimate details about her life and her past, she'll run out of here like a bat out of hell. She doesn't belong here, and she knows it."

William was angry. As a native of New Orleans, he loved the city and had no tolerance for the trashy crowd on Bourbon Street. He leaped from his chair and searched around for Elizabeth.

Meanwhile, Luke's heart was pounding. The coincidences kept surmounting. He didn't like being trapped in the center of this fiasco. And now he was being forced to drag his cousin into the middle of this mess on his wedding day. It was beginning to feel like a nightmare all over again.

Luke considered the fact that Chad had once referred to Elizabeth as "the almost Natalee Holloway." Back in 1983, Luke had almost become one of Elizabeth's rapists. Back in 1983, Natalee Holloway wasn't even born yet. Even though Luke and his friends had never actually hurt Elizabeth physically in 1983, he still seemed to be paying a price for what he *almost* did. None of this felt fair. Chad had also mentioned that Elizabeth resembled Natalee Holloway. Out of curiosity, Luke did a web search for Natalee Holloway on his phone. He began sweating much more profusely when he realized that this weekend was actually the anniversary of Natalee Holloway's disappearance.

Luke gazed across the room and saw William and Elizabeth having what appeared to be an intense discussion. He took a photo of her and sent it in a text to Chad and Eric.

***

Across the room, William pleaded, "I really don't want to ask you again. Please leave now."

Elizabeth answered "You're the groom, and if you want me to leave, I'll honor your wishes and go. However, as I've been saying all along, I came here with my husband—and I will leave with him! I'll find him, and we'll leave together. I promise that I'll get to the bottom of this. We'll talk to Catherine's parents later and find out why this happened. You can explain to *them* exactly why you asked us to leave. I want answers."

William asked curiously, "How do you know Senator Johnson?"

Elizabeth laughed. "I don't know Senator Johnson. I know who he is, but I certainly don't know him personally."

"Well, he knows you—or at least he knows who you are."

"No he doesn't. He doesn't know me, and I certainly don't know him. I just passed by him a few minutes ago. He didn't recognize me because there's no reason for him to recognize me. You're being ridiculous."

Elizabeth's subconscious was beginning to have fleeting thoughts about recent strange phone conversations. She had recently spoken to someone on the phone about a United States Senator, but it felt more like a dream. The details weren't clear. Another thought entered her mind: "Someone famous will be attending that wedding." She looked across the room and saw Senator Johnson. Most people would consider him famous. However, she couldn't think of any reason that she could possibly know him personally. Her vision became blurred for a moment. She gazed across the room, heard humming in her head, and saw tiny flashes of white light.

William finally spoke again, "Well, perhaps Senator Johnson doesn't recognize you, but his son certainly knows you. He went to your wedding."

"Are you serious? I didn't know that. He must have been there with someone from Nick's side of the family. What's his first name?"

"He wasn't invited to your wedding."

Elizabeth was confused. "Then why was he there?"

"I have no idea why he crashed your wedding. Maybe it was one of your previous marriages. How many times have you been married?"

"I've only been married once! Nick and I met in 1984. We've been married since 1992, and I've never been married to anybody else. I really do believe you have me mixed up with somebody else!"

"Nope, I do not have you mixed up with anybody else. Your name is Elizabeth, right? And your last name is Green, correct?"

"That was my maiden name."

"Okay," William said. He took a deep breath. "I asked a few people around here if they know Elizabeth Green. What's your married name?"

"Elizabeth Reed."

"I know that you're the right person because you were identified from across the room. When did you live in New Orleans?"

"How exactly was I identified? Who identified me from across the room? I have never lived in New Orleans! Wrong again. I've been there, but never lived there. Isn't that where you're from?"

"Yes, but this has nothing to do with me. When did you visit there?" William asked.

"I've only been to New Orleans a couple times. I went there when I was fourteen with my church choir."

"How long were you there?"

"A few days I think. Why?"

"What was the name of your church?"

"East Side Baptist Church, which is down in South Carolina. Again, why are you asking me about this?"

"You said you've been to New Orleans twice. What about the second time?"

"Nick and I went there a few years ago for a Tulane football game. And we saw a Saints game too."

"OK. Tell me about your father."

"My father passed away about five years ago."

"Aha!" William exclaimed. "That's exactly what Luke predicted you would say. He was right!"

"Who is Luke?"

"You know who he is. You met him a long time ago. He spoke to you on the phone recently. Don't you remember? He's here at this wedding."

"There's somebody at this wedding who knows me from a long time ago? Seriously?"

Elizabeth's subconscious was slowly putting the pieces together, but her conscious mind was still blocking out the two phone calls. Her eyes became dazed and she felt confused.

"Tell me about your father," William said.

Elizabeth couldn't understand why he was still asking questions about her life and her father. She wanted to find Nick and go home. "Before he died, he was a quiet, humble, honest, hardworking man. He was married to my mother for nearly fifty years."

"Hardworking. Where did he work?"

"He worked for Chem-Solutions for forty years—until the day he was told by the doctors that he had only three months to live. He tried to retire twice before that, but he went back to work both times. He could never adjust to retirement life."

"That sounds really boring. What did he ever do to make the world a better place?"

Elizabeth answered, "He served in the National Guard for a while. He volunteered with Habitat for Humanity. He was active in his church during his later years. He was always good to my mother." She stopped for a moment before continuing. William had asked a thought-provoking question. "William, how do I really know that he made the world a better place? I'll tell you exactly how I know that. I know that because there was a huge crowd—lines wrapped around the inside of the funeral home and out the door—when he passed away. Isn't that what's most important anyway? Isn't that what we all want? Don't we all want people to care about us? Each and every one of us should have a positive influence on as many human lives as we possibly can while we're here, right?"

William stared at her in silence.

"William, this day is about you. It's not about me or my dad.

This is about you and Catherine. And it looks like you're both already making the world a better place. You're studying to become doctors. And look at all of these people here tonight! They're all here to wish you well! Doesn't that make you feel good? I wish you both well, but you've certainly spent far too much time chatting with me about my life. I need to leave because I'm not welcome here for some reason. Isn't that right? You should probably move along and speak to some of your other guests—those who are welcome here."

Catherine walked up, and Elizabeth greeted her with a wide smile. Elizabeth reached for her hand and complimented her on her beautiful dress, the wedding ceremony, and the reception. It had been several years since Elizabeth had seen Catherine.

Nick walked over and congratulated Catherine and William. He asked where they were planning to go for their honeymoon. Catherine began to describe their upcoming trip across central Europe.

Catherine and Nick conversed like old friends.

"Nick, how long have you two been married?" William asked.

Nick replied, "In August, we'll celebrate twenty years. The key to success is to marry your best friend." Nick smiled and placed his arm around Elizabeth.

William's eyes widened.

Elizabeth added, "And we dated for eight years before we got married. We met in college—just like the two of you. You need to be sure about these important decisions in life."

William gazed at his new bride and told her that he needed to step away for a moment.

Nick wished William well as he walked away.

When another guest sparked up a conversation with Catherine, Nick and Elizabeth were left standing together, alone.

"I've been trying to find you for a while," Elizabeth began. "Something really strange has been happening here. I'm ready to leave. The groom is asking weird questions. I don't know if he's playing some sort of joke—or if he has me mixed up with somebody else."

Nick laughed. "Are you serious? You must have misunderstood. How much wine have you had tonight?"

"I didn't misunderstand, and I've only had one glass of wine."

***

Across the room, Senator Johnson tapped William on the shoulder. He was sitting next to Luke at the table.

William jumped up, gasped, and turned around to greet him with a smile.

"I really had a wonderful time this weekend. Everything was beautiful. Your bride and her entire family seem like wonderful people. My whole family wishes you well. I'm sorry that I'm the only one from my family who could make it here. We're all very proud of you, William."

"Oh, I understand. Thank you—and thank you so much for being here. Are you leaving now?"

"Yes, I've got to travel early tomorrow morning. I enjoyed surrounding myself with all of this southern hospitality. Relax next week and enjoy your honeymoon. And Luke, I'm sure I'll see you back in Washington soon. Safe travels home."

Luke stood to shake hands. "Safe travels to you as well. I look forward to hearing about Eric's trip to the Caribbean. I'll be talking with him again very soon."

As Senator Johnson walked away, Luke and William sat down again.

"Whew. We dodged a bullet!" Luke gasped.

William replied, "Maybe … maybe not. I have a different bullet coming toward me now. I need to find out exactly why I've been ejecting a friend of my father-in-law from my very own wedding reception. How will I ever explain that one?"

"Let's tell him that we were tired and tipsy and decided to play a little joke on her," Luke answered. "We don't have to give him any details. We can be vaguely specific."

"Sounds like a plan."

A little while later, William told his father-in-law that his cousin knew one of the female guests from many years ago, someone who was apparently a friend of his as well. They all decided to have some fun and play a little joke on her. "If she says anything about it, please tell her that we were simply having a little bit of fun at her expense."

Daniel replied, "Look, I'm really tired. Don't worry about it, son. I'm glad you had fun. You and Catherine need to get some rest. This has been a fantastic evening!"

The remaining guests bid the happy couple farewell and began walking out of the building. As Elizabeth and Nick walked toward their car, she heard humming in her head. She had a fleeting thought of Senator Johnson before seeing a quick flash of tiny white light in front of her face. As they drove home in the pouring rain, the memory of the conversation with William quickly faded into her subconscious.

Nick turned on the radio, and Elizabeth listened intently to the words of an old Simon and Garfunkel song: "'Neath the halo of a street lamp / I turned my collar to the cold and damp / when my eyes were stabbed by the flash of a neon light / that split the night / and touched the sound of silence."

Chapter 30
The Fork in the Road

May 2012

Chad Patterson and his wife flew into Charlotte with Eric Johnson and his wife. They had spent a long weekend in the Caribbean. At the airport, Jan and Melanie decided to go shopping.

Eric sat next to Chad and whispered, "I have something to tell you. I've been holding back all weekend because I didn't want to spoil our nice weekend together."

"What's wrong?"

"Elizabeth crashed a wedding this weekend—the same wedding that Luke and my dad attended. I didn't want to spoil your good time by telling you about it earlier."

"Oh my God! Not again! Where was the wedding?"

"It was in her hometown in North Carolina. I gave her a head's up by calling her before the wedding. I warned her that my dad would be attending. That evidently gave her the opportunity to go over there and crash the wedding. I should have never called her in this first place."

"What happened at the wedding?"

"Nothing, thank God! The groom kicked her out of the reception before anything actually happened. Revenge … finally, after all these years! I'm waiting to hear back from Luke to get the rest of the story. He texted me during the reception to tell me she was getting tossed out of the reception. I haven't heard anything since."

Chad shook his head. He called information to get Elizabeth's phone number. Her outgoing message gave all callers her cell phone number. He immediately called her cell phone.

"Hello, this is Elizabeth," she answered.

"Hey, I'm at the Charlotte airport. I can't help but wonder if you are here too? I'm looking around. I don't see you anywhere?"

Elizabeth laughed. "Who is this? Do you realize how big North Carolina is? I'm nowhere near the airport."

"Thank God!"

"Who is this?"

"We finally got you! You just had to go over there and crash that wedding, didn't you?"

"I haven't crashed any weddings. Who is this?"

"Oh, come on now. You're always showing up in places where you don't belong. I know you crashed a wedding this weekend. You're a wedding crasher!"

"No, I'm not! I went to a wedding this weekend because I was invited."

"You're just a devil woman with evil on your mind, aren't you? I think of you whenever I hear that old song. I can see a tall, dark stranger giving you what you hadn't planned." He glanced toward Eric.

Chad Patterson glanced down at his phone. He saw a new text come in from Luke. Most of Luke's texts over the weekend had been delayed due to international travel. Luke also sent a photo of Elizabeth with the accompanying text: *Is this her? She's wearing a cross necklace.*

Chad finished skimming through the texts and said to Elizabeth, "I just called you a devil woman, and immediately received a text telling me that you were wearing a cross necklace at that wedding." Chad paused and continued skimming through the texts. "And now Luke's telling us that you never worked as a prostitute in

New Orleans. Well, I tried to tell everybody that before I left Fort Lauderdale back in 1983. Nobody ever listens to me anymore!"

Elizabeth responded in shock, "Oh my God! Is this Chad Patterson? You're a psychopath! You're a rapist and a murderer! Why are you calling me? I've been having horrible flashbacks about you lately for some reason!"

"Hey, I'm not a murderer. I've never murdered anybody – not yet. When did you start having flashbacks?" Chad asked.

"I had a dream about you at the beginning of March. I haven't been able to stop thinking about that horror in Fort Lauderdale ever since!"

"March 2012?" He paused for a moment. "Well, that's about right. And here I am calling you three months later—naturally. I'll call you back. I need to figure out exactly what's going on here."

Elizabeth hung up the phone and saw flashes of light and heard humming.

After Chad read through his texts from Luke, he called Elizabeth again. "Okay, so you were an invited guest after all?"

"Why do you think I'd crash somebody's wedding?" she asked.

"You'd never do something like that, would you? You're not capable of stalking. You're not capable of crashing a wedding. I've heard it all before. I don't know what to believe. The hypnosis is over now. Do you finally remember everything?"

"What do you mean by hypnosis?"

"You don't remember anything significant about March of 2012?"

Jan and Melanie approached Chad as they returned from shopping.

"This is surreal," Chad gasped. "I need to hang up now!"

Chapter 31
The Bottled-Up Outrage

June 2012

A story in the local news grabbed Elizabeth's attention. The Jerry Sandusky sexual assault trial was dominating the airwaves, but one remark rocked her to the core. One of Jerry Sandusky's victims had remained silent for many years because Jerry Sandusky said, "Nobody will believe you." The victim knew that Sandusky was right. Speaking out about what happened to him seemed futile. Elizabeth could relate to that same feeling of powerlessness. Chad Patterson had said those exact words to her in 1983. Her chest tightened.

A few days after the wedding, Eric Johnson called Elizabeth and said, "So you're telling people about us now, aren't you? We thought you couldn't remember anything because you were stupid. That hypnosis stuff is real? Do you know what I think happened? Luke and I must have been close enough to the hypnosis ceremony that we got zapped too. Do you remember Steve? He hasn't surfaced in the past three decades, has he? That's because he must have been out on the beach or down the street somewhere when Chad did that hypnosis thing. Steve was too far away to get zapped. You've only had to deal with three of us for the past three decades—not four of us."

Elizabeth felt like a volcano about to explode. "If I ever see your face again, I'll chop off your penis and stuff it down your throat!" she shouted.

Eric Johnson candidly replied, "Wait. I need to envision that for a second. Now what's that supposed to do—kill two birds with one stone?"

"I suppose that's the point!" she shouted.

Eric whistled. "Do you see how this works? Those words you just said—they don't bother me at all. They're words. I can get through this just fine. I don't need anybody to hypnotize me so I can get through this. I can whistle right now and move along with my day. I'm fine."

"There's a huge difference between what I just said to you over the phone and four brutal thugs coming after me in real life!"

"You may have a point there, but do you realize that you just threatened me? I have access to the Secret Service! I can send them after you for threatening me like that."

"Bring 'em on!" Elizabeth screamed. Nearly three decades of anger was fueling inside of her. "I'll be more than happy to explain to them why I just said those words to you!" She slammed down the phone and immediately saw a flash of light and heard humming.

The phone rang again a few minutes later.

Chad Patterson was on the other end of the line. "The sweet little southern girl finally said the word *penis*. I can't believe it… and in that context. Your dad—when he had to deal with Eric all those years ago—should have been more aggressive. He should have stood up for you and for himself. He could have straightened us out many years ago."

"I don't know what you're referring to, but I feel like he's been helping me through this," Elizabeth answered.

"How is that possible? He passed away a few years ago, didn't he? You told us that he passed away."

"Yes, he passed away in 2007. But three months ago, before I ever realized that you were the person in my dream, I found a perfect round sand dollar on the beach in dry sand. It was like a miracle. I found it on the fifth anniversary of his death. I think that was his way, and God's way, of telling me that they were seeing me through to the end. I had no idea what was ahead of me at the time. But just like that little sand dollar, I could make it all the way to the dry sand without being broken. When I found the unbroken sand dollar, all the bad memories were still ahead of me."

"What does that feel like to have all these memories coming back like this?"

"It feels like brain vomit."

"Brain vomit?"

"Yes, when a person needs to vomit, they can't stop it from happening. They have to stop everything else they're doing and deal with it. When the memories start flowing out of my subconscious, I have to stop everything else I'm doing and deal with the memories."

"You can flush those memories down the toilet where they belong—the same way you'd deal with any other type of vomit," Chad commented.

"But that doesn't get rid of the problem, does it? You still need to know the root cause, right? The symptom is clear, but you still need an official diagnosis. Why are these memories taking over my life like this? Why now?"

"You know why...and you remember everything now, don't you? You'll start telling people about this now, won't you?" Chad asked.

"I've already told a couple of people."

"We thought you were stalking us. I called you in 2008 because I thought you'd been stalking us. I was mad at you."

"In 2008? That was only four years ago. I haven't seen or heard from you since 1983."

"Oh goodness. When you say that you remember everything, what exactly do you mean by *everything?*"

"I remember everything that happened in 1983. I remember what you and your friends planned to do to me in Fort Lauderdale."

"But the hypnosis is over?" Chad questioned.

"Hypnosis? Is that why these memories are coming back now?"

"Look, you're probably going to remember a whole lot more

than what you realize right now. And at the pace you're going, it could be next year at this time before you remember everything. You need to let it be. Let all of this be—like the song. Do you know that song?"

"Yes, I know that song by the Beatles," Elizabeth answered.

"And do you know what else? That song is about Paul McCartney's mother. Her name was Mary. The song is about her watching over him—even though she was departed. You mentioned the sand dollar on the anniversary of your dad's death. That's a sign that you need to let it be."

Elizabeth listened and thoughtfully considered his suggestion. A few moments later, they ended the conversation. And upon doing so, Elizabeth immediately saw a flash of light and heard humming.

Chapter 32
The Truth Is Stranger Than Fiction

June 2012

Elizabeth came to a new realization. It had taken three months for the memories of 1983 to return in their entirety. She understood that the memories had returned in chronological order. She felt as though she had been putting together a puzzle, and now the puzzle of 1983 was finally complete. She hoped the nightmare was finally coming to an end.

Elizabeth relaxed on her back porch on a lovely Friday afternoon. Propping up her feet, she gazed across the yard and sensed an invisible bullet coming straight toward her forehead. She sat up and watched it coming toward her with impeccable precision, landing directly between her eyes with a jolt. She immediately picked up the phone and called Molly in California.

"The memories from 1983 all came back, Molly! I finally remember everything that happened in 1983. First of all, the memories came back in chronological order."

"Well, that makes sense," Molly commented.

"But that's not all. I understand why they're all coming back now."

"Why are the memories coming back now?"

"It was planned. Chad did something at the end of the trip to help me relax and forget all the terrible things they'd planned to do to me."

"Did he hypnotize you?" Molly asked.

"Is that what you'd call that?" Elizabeth asked.

"Yes. He hypnotized you to forget."

"And he did it for a very specific time period, Molly. It was methodically planned for all the memories to return in March of 2012."

Elizabeth ended the conversation and turned on the stereo. She connected with the lyrics from Simon and Garfunkel: "Hello, darkness my old friend / I've come to talk with you again / because a vision softly creeping / left its seeds while I was sleeping / and the vision that was planted in my brain still remains / within the sound of silence."

The following week, Elizabeth contacted a colleague at the local crisis center. Elizabeth had served on the board of directors for ten years. Theresa was an assistant director and trained crisis counselors. Elizabeth wanted to speak to Theresa about the new revelations. Theresa had made a career out of crisis counseling, particularly with rape cases.

Theresa and Elizabeth met for lunch, and Elizabeth explained the entire ordeal.

Theresa listened carefully.

"Do you really think it's possible that he hypnotized me to bury the memories for exactly twenty-nine years? Is that plausible?"

"Yes, I believe it's entirely possible," Theresa replied.

"I don't understand why this feels so traumatic. Nothing really happened to me in 1983."

"Actually, something did happen to you. You were in the presence of evil, and you lived to tell about it. It's similar to what military personnel experience—the ones who are never in combat. Something happens to them even if they never experience physical violence. They are dehumanized. Their physical safety, their mere existence, was not considered relevant. Any of us can watch our physical scars heal, but mental scars are harder to monitor and heal."

"That makes sense. Do you realize that I've narrowly escaped three different rapes in my lifetime? I got involved with this organization knowing that I had experienced a home invasion back in 1985. I narrowly escaped being raped that night, but someone else was raped while she slept in my bed. And a couple of years ago, I was accosted along the river walk while I was out walking Lily. I escaped and ran away that time. And now, I'm realizing for the first time that I narrowly escaped this ordeal with Chad Patterson back in 1983. God is sparing me from this crime, in the physical sense anyway. This is crazy."

"You're right. And one more thing: Chad Patterson didn't only want to rape you. He wanted to destroy you."

Chapter 33
Can Curiosity Kill?

August 2012

On a sweltering day, Elizabeth had a lunch meeting scheduled with three coworkers. They planned to generate a list of ideas for improvements in overall efficiency for several key internal processes. Elizabeth was looking forward to it.

A couple of weeks earlier, she had begun searching online to discover clues about Chad Patterson and any criminal behavior in his life. He seemed to be living a perfectly normal life. While searching for clues, she stumbled across a book that he coauthored about mental illness. She immediately ordered it. She wanted to read his perspectives on mental illness in his own words.

She also wanted to know the identities of the other three guys. She didn't remember their names, and she wanted answers.

Before leaving for her meeting, the phone rang.

"Hello?"

"Hello, we're conducting a marketing survey. We'd like to ask a few questions about books you've recently read."

"Sure, but I only have a few minutes. I'm on my way to a meeting."

"Thank you. First, have you ordered any books online recently?"

"I usually purchase my books at Barnes & Noble. I like walking around and seeing what's new and skimming through a few books before I make a purchase."

"So you haven't ordered any books online lately?"

Elizabeth didn't consider Chad's book because it wasn't a serious read. She didn't mention the book to the market researcher.

The male voice continued, "We have a record here that you recently ordered a book from Amazon. Are you saying that you didn't order this particular book?"

"Oh! Yes, I did order a book on Amazon, but it was nothing more than a research tool."

"What were you researching?"

"I'd prefer not to discuss those details with you, and I'm in a hurry."

"Did you order it for its content or because of its author?"

"Both," she answered.

"That particular book had several coauthors. Which author?"

"Why does that matter?"

"We're looking for details about why you ordered this book. Can you please answer the question? It's important. Do you understand who we are?"

"You told me you were market researchers. I usually take the time to respond to market researchers because I work in marketing."

"Okay, I can appreciate that, but I have another question. The co-author that you're researching…is his name Chad Patterson?"

Elizabeth's heart stopped. "How could you possibly know that?"

"What are you trying to find out about Chad Patterson in that old book? It was written back in the nineties," the male voice remarked.

"I don't want to discuss this with you anymore. I need to hang up now."

"Don't hang up! Do you believe that Chad Patterson is a good person or a bad person?"

"I don't know for sure. That's what I'm trying to find out."

"We're trying to find out too. Did you learn anything new about him in that old book?"

"Not yet."

"What do you want to know about him? You can tell us. We'd like to know too."

Elizabeth was getting extremely uncomfortable. The conversation was taking a very odd turn. She had only said Chad Patterson's name out loud a few times in her entire life. She wondered if she was on the phone with a criminal investigator instead of a market researcher.

"Did he ever hurt you physically?" the caller asked.

Elizabeth gasped. "No, but he almost did." Elizabeth finally allowed the words to flow from her soul and onto her lips. This person wanted answers. "Actually, I feel lucky to be alive."

The caller's demeanor changed from inquisitive to angry. "That's exactly right, Elizabeth! You're lucky to be alive! And if I ever cross your path again, I will kill you! You will not live to tell the story. And you're stupid. You didn't realize this was me on the phone with you this whole time?"

Elizabeth's hair stood on end. A shiver ran up and down her spine as she realized that she was actually on the phone with Chad Patterson.

A different voice came on the line and said, "Elizabeth, this is Eric Johnson. Do you remember me?"

"No, I don't."

"Good God! Yes, you do! And if I ever see your face again, I promise that you will never see the light of day again! You won't be around later to proclaim how lucky you are to be alive! I'll kill you first!"

Elizabeth tried to maintain control. Now she possibly had a name for the second one. She tried to stay strong.

Chad came back onto the line. "You've got two people here who want to kill you! How does that make you feel?"

"What's your motive?"

"We hate you. Isn't that enough? You should have never ordered that book. That transaction had to be explained to a committee and to all the other co-authors, including my wife!"

"That's too bad. Tell them I'm doing research. And I don't care how much discomfort it caused you. You should have known there'd eventually be consequences for your actions when you plotted to torture and murder me back in 1983! If you hadn't done that, I would have never ordered this book!"

"I hope I cross your path again. I look forward to killing you!" Chad shouted.

"Ho hum. Your death threats are getting boring," she remarked sarcastically. Elizabeth couldn't relate to their deep level of anger. It made no sense. She had never been around anyone like these violent men. *Are they serious? Are they insane?* She asked, "Let me ask *you* a question this time. If you saw me on a crowded street and decided to kill me, how exactly would you do it? You'd have to do it in a public place because I'd never go anywhere alone with you. You'd have to kidnap me. Are you capable of that too? Tell me. How exactly would you kill me if you saw me? Do you carry a gun or a knife? Would you grab the nearest blunt object and hit me over the head? Would you strangle me? Which would it be? And how would you explain it to the bystanders?"

"You're crazy!" Chad exclaimed.

"*I'm* crazy? You called me and pretended to be market researchers—and then you threatened my life! And you're calling *me* crazy? Deflection at its finest! You're crazy—and you're thugs! You're common criminals!"

Chad spoke away from the phone, "Eric, this is what she did back in 1983. You can't just threaten her. No! She wants to know every little detail about your death threats." He came back on the line and said, "You know, most people wouldn't want to stay on the phone and listen to death threats—much less ask about the gory details. Why do you do that?"

"I'm not *most people*. I want answers. I'm curious by nature. And I'm strong too! Thank you for your call. I now understand that you haven't changed at all, and that's why I ordered the book. You wanted to know why I ordered it, right? You have your answer, and now I have mine too! I found out that you're still the same old thugs you always were!" She angrily hung up the phone. Upon doing so, she immediately saw flashes of light and heard humming. The memory of the phone call immediately faded into her subconscious.

Elizabeth had a few minutes before she needed to leave for her meeting. She desperately wanted to know the identity of the three males who had been with Chad Patterson. She could visualize their faces as the memories from 1983 surfaced in vivid detail.

She considered the fact that Senator Edward Johnson had recently attended a local wedding back in May. She remembered that one of the guys in Fort Lauderdale was the son of a prominent political figure who had connections to Ronald Reagan. At that point, her subconscious guided her to search if Senator Johnson had any sons who were near her age. When Eric Johnson's face appeared, Elizabeth immediately recognized him! She realized that his identity should have been obvious to her much sooner. She immediately called Molly and left a message.

Elizabeth was looking forward to her meeting. She had many new ideas, and she was excited to implement them. The meeting was scheduled at a casual barbecue restaurant in Wilson, North Carolina, along Interstate 95.

During the meeting, Elizabeth's cell phone vibrated. She glanced over and saw that the call was from Molly. The phone call triggered thoughts about Eric Johnson and Chad Patterson. Her eyes caught a glimpse of her coworker's plate of chopped barbecue with red sauce, and it sparked a horrid visual memory that Eric Johnson, Chad Patterson, and his friends had planned to mutilate her vagina, and they had taunted her about it. She immediately crossed her legs. In doing so, her body became tense. Her vision blurred. Any attempts to block out the grotesque visual caused her body to become cold and weak. She swayed and leaned toward the floor.

Adam, her coworker, thought she was reaching for something on the floor at first. But when he saw that her eyes were closed and her body was limp, he eased her onto the concrete floor. She was totally unconscious and pale. Her coworkers called 911.

Only one other table in the restaurant was occupied. One of the customers happened to be a nurse. She scurried over and checked Elizabeth's vital signs, which were good. Everyone was relieved.

"Could she be pregnant?" the nurse asked.

"We don't think so," Adam replied.

Elizabeth's eyes slowly opened. "I'm almost fifty years old," she said weakly.

Everyone was happy to see that she was awake.

Within seconds, she burst into uncontrollable tears. The shock and horror that more than one person wanted to destroy her was fully embedded into her subconscious. She was trying to be strong, but it was time to face the facts. Her life had been threatened. Her subconscious was fully aware of this, even though her conscious mind was still having trouble accepting it as fact.

Elizabeth was unable to sit or stand. Her physical strength was gone. Her heart was racing as she desperately tried to regain composure. She was terribly embarrassed and managed to subdue the tears into gentle sobs.

Harriett handed Elizabeth a napkin.

Adam tried to console her and commented, "The nurse asked us if you might be pregnant. I told her that you're pretty enough to be pregnant."

Elizabeth tried to laugh. "I'm too old to be pregnant."

Harriett asked Elizabeth for Nick's phone number. "Elizabeth, do you have any idea what might have caused this to happen? Is there anything more that we can tell him? He'll be worried."

"Tell him that this is about what happened to me in 1983. He'll understand. And you know about it too, Harriett. It entered my mind, and I couldn't make it stop. It must have been triggered by that phone call. I was trying really hard block it out. I'm sorry. Our meeting was going so well."

Harriett replied, "I know! You were so engaged—and the next thing we knew, you were passed out on the floor. That was really scary. But don't apologize. We were wrapping it up anyway."

The ambulance brought Elizabeth to the hospital. They ran tests, but she appeared to be in good physical health. Based on what she told them, they concluded that she most likely experienced post-traumatic stress disorder, but she would need to see a therapist to confirm the diagnosis.

Nick left work immediately to pick up Elizabeth at the hospital. He brought a friend along to drive Elizabeth's car home. Elizabeth was told not to drive for the rest of the week.

Chapter 34
The Outer Banks Reunion

September 2012

Elizabeth and several college friends visited the Outer Banks for a long weekend to celebrate their upcoming fiftieth birthdays. They stayed in a three-bedroom house at the Sanderling Resort.

A week prior to the trip, Molly called Elizabeth and asked, "Do you want to talk about your memories with everybody?"

"It's okay to talk about it, but I don't want it to dominate our weekend. It's been a few years since we all got together. We need to have fun, relax, and catch up. I don't want to dampen everyone's spirits. On the other hand, it'll be interesting to get their perspectives of the Fort Lauderdale trip in 1983 and the Washington trip in 1989."

Elizabeth didn't expect everyone to remember many details about either trip.

Caroline drove up from South Carolina and stayed with Elizabeth in North Carolina on the Thursday night before the reunion. They would meet the others at the resort the following day.

As they were preparing to leave on Friday morning, Caroline's sandal strap broke. "I'm getting rid of these sandals right now. I've already fixed these one time." She tossed them in the trash can.

She went out to her car to get another pair. She loved shoes and had a separate bag with only shoes. She frantically searched everywhere in her car, but could not find her shoe bag. She called home, and her daughter told her that the bag was sitting by the front door. Caroline had never put the bag of shoes in the car. The only pair she had was the broken sandals.

Elizabeth and Caroline didn't wear the same size shoe. Therefore, borrowing a pair from Elizabeth was not an option. Elizabeth gave Caroline a pair of Nick's flip-flops, which were slightly too big, and far too manly for Caroline's feminine taste. As they drove toward the Outer Banks, Elizabeth declared, "I predict that a shoe-shopping trip is in our near future!"

They stopped at a shoe outlet in Nags Head. After purchasing a few pairs, they tossed their shopping bags into the car and drove toward the resort.

***

Molly met Danielle and Lacey at the airport in Virginia Beach. Lacey flew in from Philadelphia, and Danielle flew in from Orlando. After loading their bags into the car, they settled in for the two-hour drive.

After half an hour in the car, Danielle said, "Lacey and I have something to tell you, Molly. We need to talk about it before we see Caroline and Elizabeth."

"What's wrong?" Molly asked.

Danielle said, "Lacey and I have both been dealing with some really heavy stuff at home. It's been a tough year for both of us, and we don't want to talk about it at the beach house."

"Why not?"

"We'd rather kick back, relax, and catch up with everybody. We're here to have a good time this weekend."

Molly had already heard these same words from Elizabeth. She wondered how everyone could possibly catch up with one another if nobody wanted to actually discuss what was happening in their lives. She was quickly becoming a dumping ground for deep, dark secrets.

"Okay, tell me what's going on with you two," Molly said.

"It's bad, and we're afraid that if we bring it up when we're all together, it might put a damper on the weekend. We don't want that to happen. We're not ready to talk about it yet."

"Tell me what's going on," Molly said.

Danielle finally explained, "There's no easy way to say it. Bob was diagnosed with Lou Gehrig's disease about six months ago. He's still getting around pretty well right now, but we've got a long road ahead of us."

Bob and Danielle had been dating for more than ten years. They had scheduled a wedding date a couple years earlier, but they eventually canceled it. Now they weren't sure when—or if—they could schedule another ceremony. Bob and Danielle both competed regularly in road races all over the globe. They didn't have any children, and they enjoyed traveling together, which often involved racing or hiking. Bob was fifty-three.

"Gosh, I'm so sorry to hear this, Danielle. How did you find out?" Molly asked.

"He lost strength in one arm. That's usually one of the first signs. We got the official diagnosis about six months ago. We think he has the type of Lou Gehrig's disease that's slower to progress. Anyway, our priorities in life are about to change. We're still trying to absorb this news."

"Are you sure you want to keep quiet about this all weekend? It might help to talk about it."

"Yes, I'm sure. I definitely don't want to talk about it. I'm still processing it myself. I really need to get away for a weekend to clear my head."

"Okay, I understand—and I'm so sorry. Let us know if we can do anything to help," Molly replied. "Lacey, what's happening with you?"

Lacey took a deep breath. "This is really hard to talk about. Tony was diagnosed with early Alzheimer's disease. He had to stop working a few months ago. I'm making plans now to go back to school for a nursing degree. Hopefully, I can learn how to take care of him, and I'll need to go back to work anyway. We've got a long road ahead of us too."

Lacey and Tony had been married for more than twenty years, and they had three children. Their oldest child had just started college. Their youngest had just started high school. Tony was forty-eight.

Molly was devastated to hear the news about both of them. Bob and Tony were vivacious and young. Bob's disease would gradually destroy his body, but his mind would remain intact. Tony's disease would gradually destroy his mind, but his body would remain intact.

Chapter 35
Breaking the Silence

September 2012

At the Sanderling Resort, everyone settled into the spacious home they had rented for the weekend. It offered views of the inlet on one side and ocean views on the other. The home was comfortable, tastefully decorated, surrounded by porches and decks for enjoying the breathtaking views.

Nearly four years had passed since all five of them had been together, although they had occasionally seen each other individually.

While unpacking their bags, Danielle observed Elizabeth and Caroline's shopping bags. "You've already been shopping today, huh?"

"I've never had a better excuse to go shoe shopping! I forgot all of my shoes. We're all turning fifty this year. I suppose that means we're getting old and forgetful," Caroline said with a laugh.

"We're not getting old! We may be turning fifty, but we're the youthful versions of fifty!" Elizabeth confidently declared.

After everyone settled in, they strolled out to the beach with chairs, towels, appetizers, and wine. They chatted until sunset.

Lacey lived in Philadelphia and had three teenagers. She had been a full-time mommy for a long time.

Danielle was working at a television station in Florida, and she brought along a photo album filled with travel memorabilia. Everyone flipped through the pages in awe of the beautiful scenery.

Molly had never married, but she had a longtime boyfriend in California. She was already semiretired and doing consulting work. She also served on the city council.

Caroline had been married for twenty years, and one of her two children was about to graduate from college. She owned a successful day-care facility in South Carolina. From the outside, their lives looked perfect as they sipped their wine and watched the waves break and roll onto the sand.

There was never any discussion of Bob's disease, Tony's disease, or Elizabeth's traumatic memories. They had too many other happy life events to discuss. They had too many other happy memories to reminisce about. They discussed going to Europe for their next reunion.

Later that evening, they walked to a restaurant tavern, which was part of the resort.

At dinner, Molly finally said, "Listen up everybody. Something's been happening with Elizabeth lately, and she wants to talk about it with us. Let me preface by saying that she doesn't want this to be a depressing subject that could dampen our whole weekend. Those are her words." Molly nodded toward Lacey and Danielle.

Lacey and Danielle glanced at one another.

Elizabeth explained what had happened on the spring break trip to Fort Lauderdale in 1983.

"Why didn't you talk about it in Fort Lauderdale—when it happened?" Danielle asked.

"It was too traumatic. I couldn't process it myself at the time. It seemed impossible to explain. I was humiliated and ashamed."

Molly stared across the table at Lacey and Danielle.

Elizabeth added, "Actually, I did try to mention it to Rebecca and Sue at first. I was never very close to either one of them. They just happened to be the first two people I saw after it happened. They didn't take me very seriously. In their defense, I didn't want to talk about it anyway."

"But since then?" Lacey asked. "That was nearly thirty years ago. Why haven't you talked about it since then?"

Elizabeth took a deep breath and looked toward Molly. She wasn't quite sure how to explain the reason for nearly thirty years of suppression.

"He hypnotized her," Molly finally announced.

"He did what?" Danielle asked.

Everyone's eyes widened, and they looked toward Elizabeth.

"It's okay to laugh … about that part anyway … but this is not a joke. I promise."

Danielle sat back and remarked, "Wait a minute. Let me get this straight. This guy and his friends threatened to do all of those horrible things to you. And after all of that happened, you allowed one of those same guys to hypnotize you so that you could forget it ever happened?"

After a couple glasses of wine, Elizabeth managed to giggle about it for the first time. "When you put it that way, it sounds ridiculous. But the answer is yes. And it actually worked for twenty-nine years."

"But you were hypnotized by one of them? Wouldn't that make it worse, not better?" Danielle asked.

"It was horrible and I wanted the memory of it to go away for as long as possible. He was an Ivy League psychology major. He was the only person around who knew how to do anything like that. He also had a vested interest because he wanted it to disappear as badly as I did."

"But what if you ran into one of them again? Wouldn't it put you in more danger if you couldn't remember them—or anything about them?" Danielle asked.

"Well, you're very astute. I never imagined I'd cross any of their paths again. Neither did they, I suppose. But now that you mention it, I actually *did* cross one of their paths again. We all did as a matter of fact. Do you remember when we all went to Washington in 1989? One of those guys came over to our table. I didn't recognize him at first. I think he must have recognized us because we were all together. That was only six years after our spring break trip."

Lacey commented, "I remember that trip, but I can't remember any details about it. My memory is not always that great."

"Ask me anything. These memories are coming back like they're happening all over again right now. I remember 1983 like it happened last week. The details are vivid. Would you like for me to describe how our motel room smelled? I can remember the scents."

Caroline interjected, "I remember our trip to Washington, but I don't remember anyone coming over to our table."

"Think about it. Why would you remember it? It was nearly a quarter of a century ago. You didn't know him. It was late at night. We'd all been drinking, and it lasted for less than five minutes. Molly had gone the bathroom. It happened while she was away from the table. It happened fast."

Danielle responded, "Actually, I sort of remember a guy coming over to our table to talk to us, but it's very vague. He said he knew us. It wasn't a good situation."

"You're all experiencing natural memory loss that occurs after a long period of time. I haven't thought about this at all since 1989. Evidently, I blocked it out immediately after it happened. But now, it feels like it just happened all over again. That's another point. The memories are coming back in chronological order. I didn't remember the 1989 experience at all—not until all the memories from 1983 returned." Elizabeth stopped and looked around the table. Everyone appeared fascinated. "You do believe me, don't you?"

"Yes, of course we believe you. It's a crazy story. That's all," Lacey said.

"I understand. This is not your average Joe sad story, is it? Nobody's ever written a country music song about this sort of thing, have they? How would that song go, exactly?" Elizabeth pretended to play a guitar. "Sing along with me now. I was traumatized, polarized, then hypnotized / to make it all disappear / for exactly twenty-nine years!"

"It helps to talk about this, doesn't it?" Molly asked. She stared towards Lacey and Danielle.

"In her case, it's been nearly thirty years since it happened," Lacey responded.

Elizabeth commented, "I must admit that this is the first time I've actually been able to loosen up about this. Last month, I passed out during a lunch meeting at work. An ambulance came and took me to the emergency room. They think I may have post-traumatic stress disorder."

The mood immediately turned somber again.

Lacey finally commented, "I'm sorry that happened. I ran into Sandy last month. I almost asked her to join us this weekend."

"No!" Molly, Danielle, and Elizabeth all cried out together.

Elizabeth remarked, "I know that I personally had issues with her, particularly on that spring break trip, but I never knew that anybody else had issues with her too?"

"She was sneaky, and sometimes a bully," Danielle said.

"I realize that now, but I didn't realize it back then—at least not until the Fort Lauderdale trip," Elizabeth admitted.

"Sandy told those guys she was a prostitute," Molly explained matter-of-factly.

Everyone was silent for a moment.

Elizabeth added, "I think it started out as a joke—or she made a sarcastic remark—but those guys took her seriously. It spiraled out of control from there. I said a few things that I didn't understand at the time. I didn't know what a red-light district was. But we can't make excuses for those guys. They had already planned their sadistic idea long before Sandy told them anything. She simply threw fuel on the flames. She trusted those guys. Heck, I trusted those guys. Everyone did. That was a big part of the danger, our misplaced trust. But they went to a strip club, and they were ready for hate-filled violence afterward."

"There were probably plenty of other times we were in danger," Molly added. "We were naïve back then."

Elizabeth looked around the restaurant. "People from

Washington like to come down here to the Outer Banks on their vacations, don't they, Molly?"

They all glanced around the room. The restaurant was extremely quiet.

"Yes, this is a popular vacation spot for people in Virginia, Maryland, and Washington," Molly answered.

Elizabeth felt short of breath for a moment. "I didn't pick this vacation spot. Don't you remember? I didn't want to schedule a trip here in September because it's the middle of hurricane season. I wanted to go to the mountains, or somewhere else."

"We know that, Elizabeth."

"And when we scheduled this trip—back in January or February—I wasn't even having the memories yet. I didn't even know who Eric Johnson was when we scheduled this trip!"

"We know that. Nobody thinks you scheduled this trip because of him," Danielle said.

When they returned to their beach house, they opened a bottle of wine and ventured out to the wooden porch. Crashing waves sounded in the background.

"Did you hear something in the bushes? Is somebody there?" Lacey stood up and leaned over the porch railing before stepping back quickly. "Just kidding," she said with a laugh.

"Those guys must realize that you never told anybody about them, right? That gives them even more power," Molly observed.

"You're right." Lacey pulled out her phone. "What's the main guy's name, the one you liked? Did you say his name was Chad Patterson? Is he on Facebook?" Lacey found a Facebook page for Chad Patterson and showed it to Elizabeth. "Is this him?"

"Yes, that's him," Elizabeth stared at the photo, trying not to react.

"Why don't I send him a private message to tell him that we all know about him now?" Lacey asked.

"I don't think that's a very good idea," Elizabeth answered.

"What about Eric Johnson? Is he on Facebook?"

"Not that I've seen, but he and his father are all over the web."

"Is this him?" Lacey handed her phone to Elizabeth.

"Yep, that's him," Elizabeth said. "Danielle, your old boyfriend was down there with us. George knew that something was going on, but he didn't know exactly what it was. I was too embarrassed to tell him or anybody else. I wanted to downplay the whole thing as much as possible."

"What did George do?" Danielle asked.

"He pulled one of them off of me at one point. I haven't figured out who that guy is yet. There were four guys. One of them grabbed me from behind and pinned me against the wall. We were on the sidewalk under a breezeway. George saw it, came over, and pulled him off of me. George screamed at him and made me feel slightly protected. He yelled at all four of them a different time."

"That sounds like something George would do," Danielle said.

"We still had another night at the motel after Chad left. The other three were just as bad, if not worse, than Chad. I was glad George was there. I felt safer with him around."

The conversation eventually subsided, and everyone got ready for bedtime.

"Make sure all the doors are locked," Elizabeth said.

They walked around the house and double-checked the locks on all the doors and windows.

Chapter 36
Four Wild Animals

September 2012

The following day, they ventured north to Corolla. Wild horses were known to roam the undeveloped natural area. Because of overpopulation, the wild horses were loosely fenced in the northernmost section of the Outer Banks. The Atlantic Ocean surrounded the twenty-five-mile piece of land.

They hiked through wooded trails and searched for the horses. They hiked through the trails for an hour, but never saw a horse. Lacey occasionally pretended to see one off in the distance. She was having fun teasing everyone, but nobody fell for it.

They finally came upon a wide-open beach with four horses trotting along the shoreline. Everyone was mesmerized as they captured photos, strolling along next to them. No one spoke. Occasionally one of the horses glanced toward them through the corner of an eye, which was thrilling.

Suddenly a pickup truck sped toward them and came to a screeching halt. The driver screamed, "Can't you read the signs? These are wild animals! They're dangerous! Stay at least fifty feet away from them!"

No-one responded to the driver as he sped away. Elizabeth thought to herself, *dangerous people don't come with flashy warning signs telling us to stay fifty feet away.*

The weekend finally came to an end. Neither Lacey nor Danielle ever mentioned their plights at home.

The following evening, Elizabeth's cell phone rang.

Molly's voice on the other line exclaimed, "Elizabeth, I have terrible news. Sit down. Bob has Lou Gehrig's disease. Tony has early Alzheimer's disease. I knew about it the whole weekend."

"Oh my God. When did you find out?"

"They told me on the way to the beach house, after I picked them up at the airport."

"Good Lord. I feel guilty right now. Did we talk about my situation too much? Why didn't they talk about it?"

"We needed to talk about your situation. They wanted an outside distraction. They weren't ready to talk about it yet."

Elizabeth understood, but was devastated as she hung up the phone.

Chapter 37
The Memory Flood

A month after the reunion, a new memory surfaced. The emotion caused her to physically lose strength. She fell back into her chair. The new memory seemed implausible, but she knew it was real. It had happened thirteen years earlier—in 1999—thousands of miles from home.

The memory of seeing Chad in England flooded Elizabeth's brain. She had kept a travel journal of that trip back in 1999. She ran into her bedroom, grabbed her travel journal, and began reading through the detailed pages. Each day's description was filled with several pages of activities, observations, and thoughts. However, on the day she had encountered Chad Patterson, she had recorded only two short paragraphs. She had made an interesting observation that day. In a restroom, someone had scratched graffiti on the wall. It stated: *Maybe this world is another planet's hell.*

Over the next several months, the memories of Elizabeth's encounters with Chad Patterson, Eric Johnson, and Luke Madison returned in chronological order – except for one memory. The memory of her father's encounter with Eric Johnson returned last. Elizabeth concluded that this was because it happened between them – not with her. She also knew very little about what transpired between them. She wondered if she would ever find out everything that occurred between the two of them.

Chapter 38
Three Grand

January 2013

As the final revelations unfolded in Elizabeth's memory, she picked up the phone and called her mother. "How did Dad's settlement turn out? After his accident, he never talked about it much."

"Oh, it went on for years. I think he finally got a thousand dollars. I think the other two guys also got a thousand dollars. A bunch of greedy lawyers were in charge. In the beginning, when he thought he was going to get a whole lot more, he set himself up with a good financial planner. The planner helped him invest much better than he had before the accident. He probably would have never aligned himself with that financial planner if he hadn't expected more from the settlement. In the end, it worked out fine. He always said that was a better way to earn the money anyway."

After Elizabeth hung up, she thought deeper about 1991 and 1992. The accident happened in 1991. Chad had mentioned that Eric crashed her wedding reception in 1992. William had mentioned it again in 2012 at his own wedding. Since then, Elizabeth had wondered how Eric found out about her wedding in the first place. *What led him there? Why had he traveled all the way to South Carolina to crash my wedding? It doesn't make sense. It seems almost too extreme—even for a person as obnoxious as Eric Johnson.* She realized he had been traveling back and forth to South Carolina for her father's case.

That was probably why Elizabeth's father consumed alcohol at the wedding reception.

Elizabeth walked over to an old armoire and pulled out her wedding video to see if she could find Eric Johnson. As she watched the video, she realized that many of her friends and family had passed away in the past twenty years. She felt nostalgic watching them all filled with life, celebrating and laughing.

Toward the end of the video, Elizabeth spotted Eric Johnson in the background. He seemed energized as she threw the bouquet. She noticed another man leaning against the doorway behind him. The visual of both of them sparked a new memory that Eric had not crashed her wedding alone. He had brought someone else along with him. She was astounded. She had possessed this video for the past two decades without ever realizing that Eric Johnson had crashed her wedding reception!

Chapter 39
Looking Back

Three Years later - January 2016

Elizabeth sipped her coffee on a quiet deck in Litchfield Beach, South Carolina. The soothing sound of ocean waves was all she could hear. No matter how many times she watched the brilliant sunlight slowly rise above the endless blue ocean, it always took her breath away. *Sunrises are one of God's great miracles.* Elizabeth was finally at peace. Nearly four years had passed without any calls from Chad Patterson, Eric Johnson, or Luke Madison.

When she arrived at the Reed family cottage earlier that weekend, Elizabeth was awestruck to see a dozen perfectly round sand dollars scattered around on the kitchen counter. Nick's stepmother, Cathy, had found them and was cleaning them. Cathy had been married to Nick's father for twenty years before his passing.

Cathy shared something important with Elizabeth that same weekend. She remembered a discussion she'd had with Nick's father many years earlier. John had told her that he ejected a couple of wedding crashers from Elizabeth's wedding reception.

This weekend was also the very first time that Cathy had found any sand dollars since John had passed away—and all of them had been scattered along the dry sand.

Elizabeth felt as though another message was being sent from above. And this time, the message came along with a dozen sand dollars. This time, the message was coming from the man who had taught her how to find sand dollars, the same man who had stood up to Eric Johnson on her wedding day.

As Elizabeth watched the sunrise, she reflected upon the significance of this miraculous weekend, as well as the turn of events over the past several years. After careful consideration, Elizabeth had finally filed a police report in 2013 for the death threats she'd received over the years. She stopped short of pressing charges, but she wanted their names on police records if something tragic suddenly happened to her. She wanted their names on police records because she knew their dangerous capabilities. And even if Eric Johnson had been convicted of making death threats against her, he would get nothing more than a slap on the wrist for the crime. Pressing charges would have felt like toying with a sleeping rattlesnake, with absolutely nothing to gain. She had explained to the police that Eric Johnson was a smart and manipulative lawyer. He was from one of the most powerful families in the world. And he had a long history of twisting the truth about Elizabeth. She filed the police report and let it be.

A new memory had also surfaced. During one of her last phone conversations with Chad Patterson, nearly four years earlier, he had told her that Eric Johnson's father knew a few things about this ongoing debacle that originally sparked in Fort Lauderdale back in 1983. Senator Johnson was extremely smart and had been putting the pieces together over the years. In what seemed to be reckless reassurance, Chad told Elizabeth that she should feel safe for as long as Senator Johnson was alive.

Elizabeth now understood that if Eric Johnson ever threatened her again, she possessed a smoking gun: the video of Eric Johnson and his colleague at her wedding reception, where he was clearly an uninvited guest. With Cathy's recent memories to validate that experience, she felt a renewed sense of peace and sanity.

The ordeal had felt surreal at times. She questioned herself along the way, but prayer helped her get through it. During the healing process, Elizabeth had considered one of her favorite prayers, the Prayer of Saint Francis of Assisi:

Lord, make me an instrument of Thy peace.
Where there is hatred, let me sow love;
Where there is injury, pardon;
Where there is doubt, faith;
Where there is despair, hope;
Where there is darkness, light;
Where there is sadness, joy.
O Divine Master, grant that I may not
So much seek
To be consoled as to console,
To be understood as to understand,
To be loved as to love;
For it is giving that we receive;
It is in pardoning that we are pardoned;
It is in dying that
We are born into eternal life.
Amen.

The prayer had moved her to send letters to Chad Patterson and Eric Johnson three years earlier, in 2013. They had never asked for forgiveness, but she had forgiven them in her heart because forgiveness was the only path to peace. Elizabeth also wrote the letters because she wanted them to fully understand that she had never stalked them. Each and every time their paths had crossed over the years was purely coincidental—except for her wedding day when Eric Johnson stalked her. And she had it on video.

The world is tiny, and their destructive reactions to crossing her path over the years needed to stop. Elizabeth tried to see things from their point of view in order to *understand* - but this was particularly challenging. She simply prayed that they had no *physical* sexual assault victims in their pasts, presents, or futures. She had added that sentiment to her letters. She would never *understand* their violent tendencies.

Upon returning home after the long weekend at Litchfield Beach in January 2016, Elizabeth received a text from Molly. It was a photo, which wasn't clear at first. When Elizabeth studied it carefully, she realized it was a photo of a perfectly round sand dollar. Molly lived near the beach in California and enjoyed walking along the shore as often as possible. Molly had just found a perfectly round sand dollar on the beach.

Chapter 40
God's Love Never Dies

The messages recently being sent from the newfound sand dollars were beginning to feel magical. Elizabeth considered a comparison that Chad Patterson had once made. He had compared the treasure of finding a sand dollar to lyrics in the Beatles song, *Let It Be:* And though they may be parted / there is still a chance that they will see. There will be an answer / Let it be. The messages were basically the same. The love that exudes from a parent never dies. The love that exudes from God never dies. Throughout the decades, Elizabeth's abusers had seemed obsessed with earthly power. But only God holds the ultimate power – which extends far beyond our earthly boundaries.

One month after the magical weekend at Litchfield Beach, Senator Johnson was found dead. He had died suddenly during his sleep. The entire country watched the story unfold on the national news.

The political ramifications surrounding his death were ongoing and controversial, particularly during an election year. However, Elizabeth could only see him as one entity. He was Eric Johnson's father.

Four months later, Elizabeth's mother passed away following a brief illness. She and Nick no longer had any living parents between them. The chapter of their lives with living parents finally came to an end.

It was finally time to move forward and let all of this be.

"And I am convinced that nothing can ever separate us from God's love. Neither death nor life, neither angels nor demons, neither our fears for today nor our worries – not even the powers of hell can separate us from God's love." Romans 8:38-39.

CONCLUSION – QUESTIONS/ANSWERS
From The Author

This final section was added to my book, based on feedback during the first six months of its original release. In looking back, I'm glad these questions were asked because this gives me an opportunity to elaborate on extremely important subject matter. Most of these questions arose from one national critique.

In my own personal experiences, as well as those I've studied and observed over the years, sexual violence, in its various forms, always has three distinct phases:

- ***Phase One: Lead-up or build-up*** – This type of crime is never random. There is always an event, or a series of events, that led to the criminal act. Even in a case where a person is spontaneously grabbed in a dark parking lot, something occurred previously to lead the perpetrator to that point. As a society, we are much quicker to judge and analyze the victim's actions before the crime – as opposed to what led the perpetrator to that point. We must look at both in order to understand the full scope of what's occurring, and therefore bring about change *before* a potential crime.
- ***Phase Two: Exertion of force*** – A perpetrator must remain in control during this second phase, and exertion of force is the vehicle to maintain that power and control.

- ***Phase Three: Aftermath*** – All three phases are important to understand, but phase three is vital to finding truth and justice. The aftermath phase involves many more people than the perpetrator and survivor. Survivors of all types of sexual violence are often blamed, shamed and doubted. And the severity of what occurred may get downplayed by outsiders. These reactions may come from family, friends, police, and lawyers. With these type of reactions, a survivor is much more likely to shut down, bury their burden, and remain silent. When this occurs, perpetrators become even more empowered.

  Denial is a very real response among survivors, as well as others in the aftermath. Denial may also cause a survivor to "block out" trauma from the conscious, but still bury the memory deeply into the subconscious, for a long period of time.

  In the aftermath phase, a survivor's attempt to remain strong and "normal" can also be misinterpreted. Human beings are all unique in how they respond to any type of violence. Survivors of sexual violence have been dehumanized and objectified. The desire to feel "human" again, after being targeted in such an inhumane way, should be acknowledged as a potential response.

  During the aftermath phase, there are two responses that will empower a person who has been violated in this manner. Say to them: 1). "It wasn't your fault," and 2). "I believe you." These two simple statements can open up dialogue, and lead everyone in the aftermath down a path toward truth and healing.

Acknowledging the above three phases lays a foundation to several of my answers. Since my book release, I've had several friends and acquaintances confess to me that their daughter, sister, roommate, or someone close to them was sexually assaulted. A few people confessed that it happened to them personally. In some cases, it happened to them more than once – in completely unrelated incidents – and sometimes years apart. In some cases, these were people I've known for a very long time, but they choose to remain silent. This crime occurs in all walks of life. No-one is immune. Yes, it's much easier to remain silent because we still live in a society where those who speak out are stigmatized. Silence cannot prevail because silence empowers predators. Silence leads to a false sense of security. Silence leads to more victims being doubted. These are the questions I've been asked, along with my answers.

1. **Why did Chad confess so much information to you, especially when he was about to leave town that same day, and would likely never see you again?**

This can be answered in one simple word: power. But I'll elaborate. When we understand that sexual violence is more about power and control, and less about sex, it makes perfect sense that he would lash out in this manner. Rape is not only a physical crime, it's a mental one. In my personal situation, their plan was meant to be a form of bullying. After their physical rape plot failed the night before, Chad lost his power and control over me, which clearly made him angry. By confessing the details of his manipulative plan to me the next day, he entered phase two of sexual violence without having the physical contact. This was his way of exuding force, and regaining power and control over me. If we could remove the word "sex" from sexual violence, we would all be better served in understanding this type of violence.

Secondly, Chad seemed to be extremely impulsive. He said to me, "The sight of you makes me sick. You shouldn't be walking around here – alive." I believe that he saw me the next day and reacted.

Thirdly, many rapists are known to enjoy instilling fear in

their victims. Even though Chad was unable to follow through with any physical violence, he seemed to find pleasure in instilling fear in me the following day. He actually stated aloud that he was enjoying our "conversation," which was terrifying to me.

Finally, when he first started lashing out, he still believed that I was a prostitute; he believed what Sandy had told him. This seemed to make him, as well as his friends, feel invincible. He thought, at the time, that he was lashing out at a prostitute. It wasn't until after he began realizing that I may not be a prostitute after all, that he appeared concerned about speaking to me in such vivid detail.

2. **Why would Chad's friends – all of whom have careers and families – bother you for decades, stalking and making "prank" phone calls?**

This question is the exact wording from a national review service. From my perspective, there are various answers to this over-generalized question, depending on the individual circumstance. Let me begin by saying that I believe Chad, Eric or Luke would be better served to answer this question because they can explain their own actions better than I – but I will respond from my perspective.

First of all, each phone call that I received from them over the years seemed to have a very specific purpose, and in some cases, that purpose was to *protect* their careers and families. Generalizing the phone calls into one question, as though every phone call had exactly the same purpose, doesn't feel like a fair question, quite frankly. But one of the primary purposes for a majority of their phone calls was that they seemed to genuinely believe I had been stalking them whenever our paths had coincidentally crossed. This clearly made them angry, and they lashed out in anger.

Secondly, each individual phone call, and the events that led to it, are explained throughout the storyline, before each call occurred. Most of the time, there were many years between phone calls. In other words, each action that they took was a direct response to a recent previous incident. They didn't simply decide on any particular day to call me, but instead called me in response to something specific that had recently occurred, such as a coincidental encounter. For example, the string of phone calls in November 2008 occurred after I had recently crossed Eric's path at a college football game. They seemed convinced that I had, not only stalked Eric at the football game, but that I had also stalked them in previous years as well. Their phone calls during that particular weekend, in November 2008, were not only motivated by misguided "revenge" for what they perceived as my stalking them, but also because they seemed to want answers.

The phone call from Eric in 2010 was made because of the news story that broke that same day. He explained that immediately.

The later phone calls in 2012, before the May wedding, were clearly made because they wanted to find out if I would be attending. And after that wedding, due to delayed text messages, they believed, at first, that I had indeed actually crashed the wedding. They eventually found out otherwise. Divine intervention became part of that experience as well, through the cross necklace.

For reasons that are still inexplicable to me, they still believed in 2008 that I had once worked as a prostitute, and possibly still might be one - even though I had been happily married for nearly 20 years - and had certainly never worked as a prostitute in the past. And they seem to have a horrible disdain towards prostitutes. Is their response normal? Of course not.

Also, the fact that we continued to cross each other's paths over the years caused their anger to escalate, and the danger therefore escalated. They often disguised their identities in the beginning of phone calls, but that seemed to be because they were trying to gather information from me. They're manipulative, and they're a toxic combination when they're together. Would Luke have ever called me on his own? I doubt it.

Finally, there was only one time in the entire book when an actual in-person stalking occurred. That happened on my wedding day in 1992, when Eric crashed my wedding reception. He seemed to genuinely believe that he was getting revenge. He seemed convinced that I had stalked him years earlier at the restaurant in Washington DC, in 1989. And later, on my wedding day in 1992, when Eric was already in town, he used the opportunity to crash my wedding reception as misguided revenge. And again, Eric clearly has a strong disdain toward prostitutes - and he still believed, at that point, that I had once worked as one. This was the beginning of his delusional, obsessive and vengeful path that lasted for decades.

A different question could be posed here. Why would a 50-year-old woman, who has been happily married for over twenty years, choose to dredge up such horrific memories – and even worse, make them public? There is only one answer: to educate and advocate.

3. *How do you know what occurred, or what was said, when you weren't there?*

I originally wrote this entire book in the order that it happened to me. In other words, the original first chapter began in 2012, when my memories first started returning - and you, the reader, learned about people, places and events at the same moments that I learned about them. The storyline originally went back and forth, from past to present, throughout the entire book. But during the editing process, I was advised that my original timeline was confusing. I was told that the story would flow much better if I would re-arrange it, and have all events unfold in chronological order. As a result of that advice, other than the first chapter, which now begins in 2016, this is ultimately what I did. All remaining chapters are told in chronological order, from 1983 through 2016. As a result of re-arranging the order of the book, I was required to place you, the reader, ahead of me throughout much of the story. By simply re-arranging the order, I was forced to tell you about other people's conversations before I found out about those same conversations. But in reality, I was provided with that same information at some other point later in the story. For example, when Chad was "confessing" his rape plot, he actually went into much more detail about their visit to the strip club. He was taunting me with vivid details. Instead of telling you those details as I learned about them from Chad, it made much more sense to give that information to you when it actually occurred – the night before. And later, after Chad left Fort Lauderdale, Eric went into much more detail about their rape plot, and their strip club visit, while taunting me along the sidewalk.

In most circumstances, I didn't repeat my revelations in the book. But in some places, I did reference a point where I learned what you, the reader, already knew. Repetition is never good in a book. Therefore, I needed to be careful not to repeat myself when l learned what you, the reader, already knew.

In a later chapter, before our Outer Banks trip in 2012, I told readers about a conversation before I ultimately found out about it. Lacey and Danielle told Molly that they didn't want to discuss their husbands' terminal illnesses during that weekend. I wasn't there when their original conversation took place, but I received all the details later. I felt that their reluctance to discuss their plights at home was significant to this overall story. They wanted to continue burying their burdens as I was finally unloading mine. I wanted you, the reader, to understand this ongoing dynamic during the Outer Banks weekend - as I was breaking my silence.

4. **Why did you collude with Chad on choosing a date for memories to return?**

Now that I'm in my 50's, I can look back at my 19-year-old self and know that I would have handled this situation much differently at age 50! At age 19, I only wanted one thing: I wanted the horror to disappear for as long as possible – preferably forever. I didn't care how the horror disappeared. I simply wanted the "problem" to go away. I felt branded, ashamed, traumatized and isolated.

Secondly, I was in denial. The horror of the past 24 hours wasn't fully processing at age 19. I still wanted desperately to trust Chad because of initial denial. As a society, we are willing to accept initial stages of denial pertaining to other types of trauma, such as death or illness of a loved one. But I don't think we've fully grasped this concept as it pertains to sexual trauma. I was traumatized, and therefore in denial of the level of danger surrounding me.

Thirdly, I placed a great deal of blame on myself. In fact, back in 1983, I blamed myself more than I blamed anyone else. In looking back, I remember feeling as though I actually deserved what was happening. Why did I feel this way? I suppose it's because I had been intimate with Chad, and he and his friends seemed convinced that I deserved their abuse. My self-esteem during that experience was depleted. And afterwards, when I made the smallest attempts to alert anyone, their spontaneous natural response was to ask questions about my actions as opposed to anyone else's actions. At age 19, "Why?" was an unsurmountable question that was being asked of me. Outsiders wanted to know *what I did* to cause this "problem." Any attempts to answer felt shameful, and therefore caused me to blame myself. The entire ordeal was inexplicable to me at the time. How could I possibly explain it to anyone else? Silence was much easier. The idea of not having to think about the horror for the next 29 years felt magical. It felt as though Chad was offering to remove poison from body. It didn't matter at all that he was the one who had actually "poisoned" me.

Finally, I believed Chad when he told me that he didn't know how to suppress the memories forever. He only knew how to make them disappear for a very specific time period. Our decision to choose that specific date, March of 2012, is explained throughout several paragraphs.

5. ***Why did you stay on the phone and have conversations with them when they called?***

First of all, my response to them varied slightly, depending on whether the conversation occurred before March of 2012, or after that time. But in all cases, I desperately wanted answers, which was the foundation for staying on the phone with them, no matter what the circumstance. Also, throughout my working life, I've spent a great deal of time on the phone with people I've never met. After decades of doing this, it feels natural to remain on the phone during uncomfortable conversations. But that's just the beginning of my answer to this somewhat complicated question.

During phone calls that occurred before March of 2012, the first moments I realized who they were, either consciously or subconsciously, I instinctively believed that I was hearing from them for the first time since spring break of 1983, which didn't make sense to me. And after staying on the phone with them, whether for a few minutes or for much longer, more memories gradually returned – memories beyond 1983. And at that point, my desperation for a deeper level of understanding became overwhelming. Not only did I *not* want to hang up, I wanted to stay on the phone for as long as possible because I was gathering information. But unfortunately, before March of 2012, the memories would quickly fade back into my subconscious when the conversation(s) ended – because of the hypnosis. All memories eventually returned, and remained intact, beginning in March of 2012.

In addition, during the conversations before March of 2012, I believe the hypnosis played a role in how I responded to them – and possibly how they responded to me. Looking back at the long phone conversation with Chad in November 2008, I felt like I was in a trance. My mind kept converting back to believing he was a "kind distinguished gentleman," which is exactly how he stated I would remember him. I do believe that divine intervention ultimately played a role in finally getting through that conversation with him in 2008. When I responded about "the sign of the cross," it felt like mental exorcism. I didn't feel like I was in total control of what I was saying. Some people believe that hypnosis is an invitation to Satan. And Satan can be combatted with the sign of the cross.

Later in 2010, Eric made a statement that he "felt hypnotized," and I know he meant it. During the phone conversation with him in May 2010, I was able to describe the ongoing hypnotic experience through the "tent" analogy, which certainly came from my subconscious! Prior to that explanation, Eric mentioned "the sign of the cross," and I immediately gained a sense of clarity like never before. When I remembered the tent analogy years later, I felt like the description was coming from someone else instead of me. But I knew the tent analogy was accurate.

After March of 2012, when memories were finally remaining intact, although these memories were always vague in the beginning, my response to their phone calls became quite different. I was much angrier, and I did hang up on them several times. I felt "less hypnotized."

Was I afraid of them during the phone calls? Yes, of course I was. Some people refer to my various responses as courageous, but I'm not sure if that was always the case. But if I was indeed courageous, please consider this old Mark Twain quote, "Courage is resistance to fear; mastery of fear – not absence of fear."

About the Author

Nicole Saint-Clair has been married for over twenty years, and has lived in several locations throughout the Carolinas. She earned a Bachelor's degree in Journalism from the University of South Carolina, and a Master's degree in Management from Southern Wesleyan University. She served on the Board of Directors for a rape crisis center for over ten years. This is her first book, which is based on true events. A portion of its profits will be donated to organizations that fight violence against women.

Printed in the United States
By Bookmasters